I SOLD MY GOLD TOOTH FOR GAS MONEY

True Tales to make you Laugh, Chortle, Snicker and Feel Inspired

Edited by Matt Jackson
Summit Studios

Library and Archives Canada Cataloguing in Publication

I sold my gold tooth for gas money : true tales to make you laugh, chortle, snicker and feel inspired / edited by Matt Jackson. -- Canadian ed.

ISBN 0-9734671-4-2
    1. Canada--Description and travel--Humor.   2. Voyages and travels--Humor.
3. Travelers' writings, Canadian (English) I. Jackson, Matt

PN6178.C3I3 2006   917.104'7   C2006-902510-X

Designed by Kirk Seton, Signet Design Solutions
Printed and bound in Canada

SUMMIT STUDIOS
#105, 2572 Birch St.
Vancouver, British Columbia
V6H 2T4 Canada

www.summitstudios.biz

This book is dedicated to all travellers who

venture forth bravely and come home

with stories to share.

Table of Contents

Introduction

By Matt Jackson

I'm sitting at my desk in Vancouver trying to write the introduction to this book. Bloody hell. I've been trying for two weeks now.

Instead, I'm gazing out my office window, dreaming of a two-week canoe trip on the Northwest Territories' South Nahanni River. I'll be leaving for the Nahanni in four weeks, and images of steaming hot springs, misty waterfalls, and soaring canyons that rise more than four thousand feet above the river are running rampant through my imagination.

Oh yes ... the book. I have to write an introduction.

While daydreaming about exotic destinations is something every traveller can relate to, I think it's fair to say the mental images we create are often deceiving. Glossy tourist brochures lead us to imagine lush rainforests without mosquitoes, or perfectly manicured beaches with more palm trees than people. We envision road trips without flat tires and indigenous cuisine without food poisoning.

In the case of the Nahanni, I'm giving little thought to the gruelling portages, dangerous whitewater, and cold mountain rain that can turn to snow at any time of the year. Some of these things will undoubtedly be part of my trip, too.

I'm convinced that a little self-deception is okay and that travel planning has to be like this. Otherwise, many people would never leave home. Even when events don't work out as envisioned, a good story almost always follows. And though we would never plan to get sprayed by camel barf in front of the Egyptian pyramids, or perform a dance that resembles the Macarena after encountering a tiger snake in Australia, we know these stories will give us plenty of fodder to use at cocktail parties.

After all, everybody loves a good story.

That is what this book is about—sharing good stories. My intention while compiling it has been to celebrate the spirit of discovery that inspires us to deceive ourselves with these perfect images and leave home, despite the inconveniences and discomforts we know we will face. This book also salutes those travellers who've had the gumption to put on a brave face and smile when things go terribly wrong.

Some of the misadventures and faux pas our contributors write about involve simple misunderstandings, like Conor Grennan's efforts to order breakfast in Ecuador in his piece "Lost in Translation." The circumstances in others are hardly believable. I absolutely love the story of what happened to Lucia Martin when she got between a lovesick rhino and the object of his affections at the San Diego Zoo.

I should also mention that in an effort to give the book greater depth, I've tried to include more than just funny anecdotes. The stories range from the heartwarming to the absurd to the inspiring.

If there is a common thread, it is serendipity. Each writer has been forced to confront the unexpected and then adapt.

One of my favourites is "Hobos at Large," a classic tale of two young men pursuing a con man across Canada by hitchhiking and hopping freight trains in the late 1940s. Another is a touching chronicle by Sharon Fitzsimmons called "Kima," which tells the story of an orphaned monkey she and her husband Doug adopted while travelling through Africa. Yet another, "Rhein in Flames" by Keith Slater, tells the tale of a European river cruise from hell.

I would like to leave you with an anecdote I heard a couple of years ago while visiting Kelowna to promote a new travel book. I was being interviewed by John Michaels on CKOV-AM's morning radio show, when a listener called in with a story I will never forget.

The incident happened while he was working at a remote roadhouse in Canada's Northwest Territories, not far from the Nahanni River. His brother-in-law was visiting, so he decided to take a day off from work to go for a walk in the bush just off the Liard Highway, which itself is nothing more than a pot-holed gravel track that runs for several hundred kilometres between "nowhere" and "further from nowhere."

A couple of hours into the hike, the men stumbled upon two backpacks with Swiss flags sewn into the fabric, two pairs of hiking boots, and a video camera stacked neatly beside the trail. They were puzzled because it wasn't the kind of place that attracted tourists; it was mostly locals who knew about and used the trail.

The strangest part was the boots. How could hikers forget their boots? Whom did they belong to? How could they walk anywhere without footwear? And more to the point, why would they leave all of that expensive gear behind?

The hikers' questions were answered five minutes later at the edge of a sunny clearing. There, presumably, were the owners of the boots. Without boots on. Without *anything* on. Making love in the sun-dappled meadow. The man and woman had no inhibitions about expressing their amorous feelings, content that they were alone in Canada's great northern wilderness.

The couple hadn't noticed the hikers, which left the men with a bit of a dilemma. What does travel etiquette say you should do in a situation like this? Continue walking across the meadow, giving a feeble nod to the couple as you pass them on the trail? Or call out from the edge of the forest and watch them scatter like soldiers under fire?

As it turns out, the caller and his friend had a better idea. They quietly backtracked to the couple's equipment, grabbed their video camera, and discreetly shot several minutes of steamy footage from the edge of the meadow. Then they returned the camera to where they had found it and departed, leaving the lovers with a little travel souvenir.

One can imagine the couple showing video footage to friends and family at a later date, only to have their travel narrative interrupted by a short adult film sequence starring themselves.

So much for being alone in the wilds of northern Canada. When it comes to travel, I guess appearances can be deceiving.

I Love Alberta Beef

How to celebrate Canada Day in Mad Cow Country.

By Kyle MacDonald

Alberta. 2003. It was the summer of two competing phenomena: the "mad cow" crisis and the bumper sticker. The American government had stopped Canadian beef from trucking across the border, but Albertans fought back with the "I Love Alberta Beef" bumper sticker campaign. It seemed as though every driver in the province had slapped a sticker to the tail end of their Chevy, Ford or Dodge. Their message was simple: Eat more beef. And love it.

It was Canada Day when I arrived in the festive mountain town of Banff with two friends, Rob and Fiddy. Bumper sticker mania was at its pinnacle. Our initial stroll through town landed us at the official "Alberta Beef" information booth. A jovial rancher in a cowboy hat and boots handed each of us a large stack of the "I Love Alberta Beef" bumper stickers with one condition: "Do you boys promise me that you'll spread the good word?"

I shook his hand, looked him straight in the eye, and replied, "Yes sir. Yes we will."

I was an oil rig worker; Rob and Fiddy were tree planters. The transient nature of our employment made this the single weekend of the summer that we crossed paths. Since it was Canada Day, we decided that we would let our hair down even further than we normally did. We decided that this weekend was going to be *the* weekend of the year. After all, it was Canada Day. Anything less would be unpatriotic.

The best way to accomplish this task, we decided, was by drinking a copious amount of beer. Normally, a ten-minute drive to the liquor store would have been all that stood between us and a weekend for the ages. But not that day.

The normally calm and relatively traffic-free streets of Banff were engulfed in a traffic snarl that would strike fear into the heart of a New York cab driver. The Canada Day parade was about to start. Banff Avenue was shut down from end to end, rendering the entire street system utterly useless to vehicle traffic. After wasting half an hour looking for a parking spot—*any* parking spot—we conceded defeat.

Rob said it best: "You know what? I'm choked. We got beat by a parade. If there was a fire and they had to shut the streets down? Maybe. A hostage situation? No problem. But a *parade*? It's such a lousy reason for not being able to buy beer."

"I know," agreed Fiddy, "but I'm not walking all the way across town and back just to buy a case of beer. Not in this heat. The temperature is supposed to top thirty *above* today."

I couldn't stand it any more. This was supposed to be *the* weekend of the year. The last thing that was going to stop us from cutting loose for Canada Day was a parade—let alone a parade that we weren't involved in.

Then it hit me: The parade! I looked at the two dejected souls next to me and asked, "You guys still have your 'I love Alberta Beef' bumper stickers?"

"Yeah, why?" they asked in unison.

"Go get all of them."

My plan would solve every problem we faced. We could get some beer, avoid walking, settle our score with the parade ... and most importantly, fulfill our promise to the rancher.

"What are we doing at the start of the parade route with all these stickers?" Rob asked.

"Watch this," I replied. I extended my arm and raised my thumb in a classic hitchhiker's pose.

Rob smiled at me and said, "Yes sir. Yes we will."

A line of classic cars started the parade. The driver of the first car raised his eyebrows high, clearly communicating that there was no possible way we would ever set foot in his vehicle, period.

The second driver somehow managed to raise his eyebrows even higher. Was my plan doomed to fail?

What we saw next made our jaws drop. Rolling toward us was a convertible like the one JFK had been assassinated in. If there was a perfect car for this moment in time, this car was it. A driver decades younger than the eyebrow-raisers asked the obvious question: "You guys need a ride?"

"Yes sir. Yes we do."

We climbed in and sat in the back of the convertible as it rolled down Banff Avenue. We were in the parade.

In a state of shock after our sudden good fortune, we played it cool for the first few minutes and got to know our driver and his two female companions. It turned out that all three worked for the same landscaping company. I glanced at the fingernails of the girl sitting beside me; they were dirty, so these people were obviously telling the truth.

I asked her, "So if you three work as landscapers, do you cut grass?"

"Yeah, why?"

"Do you cut that grassy knoll over there?" I asked, pointing to our left.

She extended her dirty fingernail and said, "That knoll? Sure, I cut it yesterday."

"Hey, Fiddy!" Rob chimed in. "Isn't that *your* grassy knoll?"

"Yup. That's the one."

"*Your* grassy knoll?" the girl asked, firing a confused glance back at Fiddy.

Fiddy filled her in: "Last night I was walking back from the bar and I decided that your grassy knoll over there was the perfect place to spend the night. So I slept there, face down, and this morning an old guy in a Buick pulled up beside me and honked his horn. Repeatedly. He was either afraid I was dead or he was offended that I had passed out on his neighbour's lawn. It was the most comfortable grassy knoll I've ever slept on."

She blushed and shot an even more confused look at Fiddy. Then she responded in the only way possible.

"Thank you," she said.

Alas, if only they had fallen in love "at first knoll." They could have shared a lifetime of blowing people's minds at cocktail parties when asked how they had met.

After dreaming for a moment about cocktail parties, I snapped back to reality. If I had the nerve to hitchhike in a parade, in the back of a JFK-assassination-style convertible driven by a guy who had a personal grassy knoll groomer (also present), I needed to take things to the next level.

"Bodyguards!" I shouted. "Quick! Front corners! Haven't you seen the movie *In the Line of Fire*? You guys need to protect me and Jackie O!"

I was butchering real history and film history in one fell swoop. But what did I care? I was in a parade. With stickers. With Jackie O.

Fiddy and Rob jumped from the slowly moving vehicle and ran to the headlights. They placed one hand on the car and the other on imaginary earpieces, listening for intelligence reports of gunmen. From my gunfire-luring perch in the car, I cheerily handed out bumper stickers to everyone who approached our heavily guarded "float."

We saw the hat first, then the eyes. There was no mistaking who it was. On top of the grassy knoll stood the man we knew would arrive. He emerged from the shadows and raised something to his shoulder. His fist. Another silhouetted shape moved to his other shoulder. His other fist. He watched coolly as we distributed hundreds of bumper stickers to hundreds of innocent people. Then he thrust both fists into the air and shouted, "Go get 'em, boys!"

It was the rancher.

We rounded the corner into the home stretch. Spectators packed the sidewalks ten deep along Banff Avenue, and others stood on the tops of buildings, shouting with delight. It felt like a tickertape victory parade.

A sudden onslaught of out-thrust hands dwindled our sticker supply down to the very last sticker. Fiddy, thinking on his feet both literally and figuratively, ran to the center of the street and hatched a plan on the spot that would decide the lucky recipient of our final sticker.

He shouted clearly, hushing the crowd: "Ladies and gentlemen, in my hands I have the final 'I Love Alberta Beef' bumper sticker that we will hand out today. I will give this sticker to the first person to come out here and show me a 'beef dance!'"

With gusto, a middle-aged mom burst from the crowd into the middle of the street. She nailed a perfect rendition of that Russian dance where you cross your arms and kick out your feet. If there was ever a perfect "beef dance," this was it.

Sticker-less but still in the spotlight, I stood up on the back seat of the convertible and addressed the crowd on the left side of the street. I shouted out what any sensible person would shout out in my situation: "Give me a *B*! Give me an *E*! Give me an *E*! Give me an *F*!" Then I cupped my ear to the crowd and shouted, "What does that spell?"

"BEEF!" the crowd shouted back.

I turned to the other side of the street. "C'mon, right side of the street, you can do better than them! Give me a...."

What followed was the first time in the history of the world, ever, that two sides of a parade route tried their best to out "beef" chant each other. There was no question the crowd had beef fever. We were spreading the disease.

Up to this point, we had made it down the parade route unmolested, handed out all the bumper stickers, and even incited a round of competitive 'beef' chanting. The crowd was clearly in the palm of our hands.

Somehow, Rob got his hands on a corrugated plastic sign with the word *Monday* printed on one side and *Tuesday* printed on the other. Seizing the opportunity, he held it over his head and shouted to the left bank of spectators, "Who likes Mondays?"

"MONDAYS!" the left bank roared back.

He turned to the right side, shouting loudly, "Who likes Tuesdays?"

"TUESDAYS!" screamed the right bank.

What followed was the first time in the history of the world, ever, that two sides of a parade route tried their damnedest to out "Monday/Tuesday" chant each other.

For the record, Tuesdays won. They always do.

With the important matter of Monday versus Tuesday settled, we bowed to the crowd and exited stage right. We were now at the end of the parade. Our classic-car-owning landscaper-cum-chauffeur pulled up to the liquor store and thanked us for an unforgettable parade experience. We thanked *him* for an unforgettable parade experience.

We bought our beer and walked back outside. Blocking out the sun was the unmistakable figure of the rancher. His weathered face broke into a wide smile as he offered us his meaty right paw.

We took turns shaking it firmly while he looked us square in the eyes. "We did our best to spread the word," I said, grinning from ear to ear.

"Yes boys. Yes you did."

Originally from Belcarra, British Columbia, Kyle MacDonald has planted more than 100,000 trees and delivered more than 1,000 pizzas, but has eaten only one scorpion (don't ask!). When he is not promoting Alberta beef in Canada Day parades, he is stealing flags from the Prime Minister's office (again, don't ask!). He loves standing on street corners in Montreal, where he hawks copies of shoddily-bound English literature to Francophones in sub-zero temperatures. His current publisher is Kinko's.

Lost in Translation

Why does ordering an apple Danish have to be so difficult?

By Conor Grennan

The first person I spoke to upon arriving in Quito was the woman at the airport tourist desk. I had flown all the way from the United States to do some cycling in Ecuador, and I now needed to find a hostel for the night and figure out how to get my bike into town. The chain had been hopelessly twisted on the long flight, and it needed repairing. The woman was kind and very helpful; she called the hostel, booked me into a room, and told me where I could find a van to transport my now useless bike.

If I had known then that this nice lady is the only person in Ecuador who speaks English, I probably would have hung out at the airport for a while, chatting about myself. In my ignorance, however, I walked outside, loaded my gear into a waiting van and headed into Quito.

I arrived at the Hostel Varama in an area known as New Town at around nine-thirty in the evening. A guy in his early twenties unlocked the door and showed me to my room—the most expensive one in the place was ten American dollars per night. Ecuador evidently decided to give up their own currency a few years ago and adopt the US dollar. They do, however, mint their own coins; thus, instead of Thomas Jefferson on the nickel you have Juan Montalvo, who, like his American counterpart, must have invented something as timeless as the dumbwaiter.

It wasn't too late at night, so I would normally have gone for a walk to stretch my legs—but not in Quito. No sir, the Lonely Planet guide assured me that if I walked out the door in Quito after sunset, I would immediately be attacked and murdered. Not only that, the thief would steal my identity and return to the US to spend Christmas with my family and arrange to meet up with my ex-girlfriends. Just a quick drink for old time's sake, you know.

I wasn't real anxious to let that happen (though it would make one hell of a story), so I decided to stay inside and take it easy. I was tired after my long trip anyway, and felt absurdly jet-lagged. I sat down with a pen and paper and calculated that my body clock was now set to about late June 2020. I tried going to sleep, but woke up every fifty-five minutes, which is apparently how people sleep in the future.

I woke up early the next day, eager to have a look around Quito in the safety of daylight. The first order of business was to move my bags to the five-dollar room down the hall, the one that was large enough for a single bed and maybe a handful of peas. I didn't have any peas, and was thus hoping to spread out a bit.

I informed the young guy who was running the place that I wanted to switch rooms, and quickly discovered that he spoke no English. It took some convincing to get him to follow me upstairs so I could show him what I would be doing, and presumably, get him to give me a key to the other door. He had a wary look in his eye, and I finally had to physically take his arm and lead him upstairs to show him I was changing rooms. What he could possibly have been afraid of is beyond me, though it probably didn't help that I was barking out various combinations of the four Spanish words I knew like a disturbed parrot. It probably didn't help either that in seeking the door key to the new room, I used the word "muerte" (death) instead of "puerta" (door), and that my miming of a turning key may have looked, in context, like I was planning to gut him like a hog.

In the next hour of wandering around, I quickly discovered that the good people of Quito do not speak English. And really, why should they? I found this to be rather exhilarating, like this was real travelling somehow. If nobody was speaking English in the backpacker quarter of the capital, they certainly wouldn't in the rest of the country—I had no choice but to learn some Spanish if I wanted to eat. And I *really* wanted to eat. Right then, in fact. So I headed off to find some breakfast.

I quickly discovered that there is not a whole lot of choice at 8:00 a.m. in Quito, but the neighbourhood was quite pleasant. Walking west toward Old Town, you trundle through narrow streets that roll along with the hills, rising to the north, falling to the south, as if the whole city were on a swaying ship. There is so much whitewashed, colonial architecture to catch your eye that you don't even notice the grand old plazas until you burst into them like a clearing in the woods. I had just traversed one, the *Plaza de la Independencia*, shaded by tall palm trees and lined with stately colonial-era arcades, when I found what I was looking for: a small café that was selling a variety of pastries, most of which looked quite appetizing.

I wandered in and perused the glass case until a man with a large smile greeted me, no doubt asking what I wanted to eat. This being my first Spanish conversation in Ecuador, aside from the rather unsuccessful one at my hostel, I think it is worth describing here.

Now, if I had wandered into a café in, say, northern China, the process of buying a pastry would be fairly simple. The man behind the counter would take one look at me, know that I had a better chance of juggling giraffes than speaking Chinese, and would move straight to mime, pointing at things, so that I could nod or shake my head as warranted. But this was not China, this was Ecuador, and that completely altered the equation.

In Quito, people simply assume that you speak Spanish, even if you are American (in fact, especially if you are American), and that confidence is rather contagious. I just did not to want to let this friendly chap down, and it was inspiring the way he spoke to me as someone with equal or superior Spanish to himself. From the first moment, I had myself believing that I knew exactly what he was offering me.

That's when things started to spiral out of control.

I do not wish to sound as if I am passing judgment on the 330 million people who claim Spanish as their first language, but I would appeal to any etymologists out there to explain how you get "naranja" from "orange," as they have done in Latin America.

It doesn't make any sense. You know what "orange" is in French? "Orange." In German? That's right, "orange." How about Swedish? Go on, have a guess. Give up? Well, folks, you can look it up: "Orange." So what's up with Spanish?

Unable to locate anything on the board that resembled "orange juice," I took a stab at one of the other word combinations up there. I received for my efforts a set of raised eyebrows accompanied by a super thick yogurt drink that tasted remarkably like bean dip.

And then there was the meat pie/apple Danish mix-up. This was especially irritating, because I'm sure I pointed to an apple Danish. The guy behind the counter must have made some sleight of hand while pointing. Not to trick me, you understand, but because that's probably how the conversation went, which is to say, his end of the conversation. He was speaking a great deal, and I was simply smiling and nodding a lot.

Let me paint you a picture, as this would certainly repeat itself over the next few months.

I point to an apple Danish and he says (in indecipherable Spanish), "I see that you are pointing at an apple Danish. That certainly makes sense, as it is eight o'clock in the morning. Apple Danishes are universally considered breakfast food, even here in Ecuador. There is no other logical choice, to be sure. You are certainly going to enjoy this particular pastry—it is one of my personal favourites. You would have to be crazy to order, say, a meat pie at this hour." I would nod enthusiastically, which for some reason would throw him off.

"What? You want a meat pie? You do not actually want a meat pie, do you?" he would say. I, of course, would just continue to nod.

"Wait a minute, perhaps I have unfairly leapt to conclusions," he would continue. "I have been guilty of this in the past, and it has brought pain to those closest to me. I will not repeat such an error now. Please tell me sir, are you in fact saying that you want a meat pie, rather than this delicious apple Danish, for breakfast? This is what you eat in America?"

Nod, nod, nod.

"Well, then, meat pie it is. I shall happily serve this to you, my friend. It seems strange to me, but I will not judge you or your culture. And it will probably taste rather nice with the bean dip you ordered."

So I got the goddamn meat pie. And worse yet, every non-Spanish-speaking American who wanders in there for breakfast, nodding dumbly, will now get a meat pie as the default choice.

All I can do is apologize in advance.

Conor Grennan is an Irish American who spent eight years working in international public policy in Prague and Brussels before taking eighteen months off to travel the world. His work can also be found in the travel humour anthologies What Color is Your Jockstrap *and* Tales from Nowhere, *as well as on his web site, www.conorgrennan.com. He is fluent in one language.*

I Sold My Gold Tooth for Gas Money

Sometimes a guy gets desperate.

By Michael Glinz

Mary came to me in a vision one morning while I was lying in bed praying the rosary. Radiating love and purity, she told me to follow her son. But before Mary could elaborate any further, she disappeared. Where was her son going? What did he want me to do? And how was I supposed to follow him without a little more insight?

I was in my early twenties at the time. Although I was a handyman by trade, I had been working for a limousine company in Calgary, Alberta, shuttling celebrities and rich businessmen around town. The tip money was great. The only problem was that I would spend my tip money almost as quickly as I made it. After work, I often stopped at a casino on the way home, hoping to run up my daily earnings. It never happened. What started as harmless fun soon turned into an all-consuming addiction.

It wasn't long before I started attending church to confess my sins and search for answers. It was here that I met a fellow named Scally, who spent several hours a day praying in the church.

When I told him about my vision of Mary, his eyes bulged with excitement. "You have to tell the priest about this!" he exclaimed.

I wasn't so sure, but Scally kept nagging at me until one afternoon I broke down and mentioned it to one of the priests. I told him about the dream and about Mary's instructions to follow her son.

"What does it all mean?" I asked him.

The priest looked as confused as I was, and obviously wanted nothing to do with this lunatic in front of him. He stared blankly at me and told me to go and see Father Francois.

Father Francois was a kind older gentleman, and when I had finished relating my story to him, he gave me an understanding pat on the shoulder. "My son, what do you do for a living?" he inquired.

I didn't want to tell him about my job as a limousine driver, so I told him I was a handyman—it sounded much more industrious.

The good Father pondered my answer, and then came up with a suggestion. As luck would have it, he was in charge of maintenance for all of the Catholic parishes in Canada's Yukon Territory. "We are in great need of somebody with your skills," he said. "If you truly want to follow Mary, my son, you can go to the Yukon and help us refurbish our churches."

When Scally found out what I was planning to do, he told me that he was coming along. So we loaded my little Ford hatchback with so much stuff that its tires practically rubbed against the wheel wells. It was blessed by Father Francois, who exorcised it of all demons. And, thinking it couldn't hurt, Scally poured holy water into the radiator.

So it was that on a warm summer day in late June, Scally and I found ourselves saying farewell to our loved ones. My girlfriend Donna was sad to see me go, though Scally's wife seemed more perplexed than anything. Scally was married with two children, and although he was only traveling with me as far as Whitehorse, he hoped to move his family to northern Canada over the next few months.

"The Holy Spirit lives in the Yukon," he told me rather matter-of-factly.

For the next three days, the only time Scally wasn't praying the rosary was when we were eating. It was the most boring road trip I've ever taken.

Not far from the British Columbia border, we stopped for several days to overhaul the plumbing in a small Catholic church just west of Watson Lake. From there it was another five hundred kilometres to Whitehorse, where I dropped Scally at the airport.

I was glad to get rid of Scally—his spiritual exuberance was a bit much, even for me. I could finally sit back, set the car on cruise control and enjoy the boundless scenery as it drifted past. Between Whitehorse and Dawson City, the North Klondike highway cuts between rolling green mountains cloaked with conifers, dipping every so often into a broad river valley like the Stewart or the Pelly. Everything was so remote. Perhaps that's why it was so beautiful.

About the time I hit the Stewart River, I bit down hard on a rocklike piece of caramel and a searing pain shot through my mouth. When I reached in and plucked out the offending piece of shrapnel, my $1,500 gold filling was stuck to it. The caramel had ripped the filling right out of my mouth, titanium screws and all. The only thing I could do was put the filling in my pocket for future reattachment.

When I finally reached Dawson City, I met the bishop at the church, and he took me to see Father Leo, who was an old military chaplain. Father Leo had grey hair, but was in trim condition. What was most noticeable about the good Father, however, was his ring and watch. Both of them were laden with all kinds of gold nuggets, which he had presumably received from local miners.

It took me a few weeks to work up the courage, but eventually I asked him: "If you've dedicated your life to God, why haven't you donated your ring and watch to Jesus?"

"I didn't take the vow of poverty," was all he said, but not without a faint trace of a smile.

The good Father had a house with a small ten-by-ten-foot cabin in the back yard, which is where I lived for the next several weeks. During the days, I worked doing maintenance on the church. I cut down weeds, painted and whitewashed some of the buildings, and on one occasion, I hauled two semi trailers' worth of wood and piled it in the basement of the church. For three days I walked up and down those endless stairs.

I even restored a small gravesite that belonged to the famous Father William Judge, the first doctor in the Yukon to trade medicine for services. If a miner or trapper was injured, he would give them medicine in return for labour—and that's how he built the local hospital.

All this work kept me occupied during the day, but every evening I returned to my lonely cabin. Inside there was nothing more than bunk beds and a wood-burning stove that made what seemed to me a plaintive hissing noise. Although it was only mid-August, the cabin was already getting very cold at night, and the lack of company made it worse.

Then there was another sound that I came to know all too well. About twenty paces from my cabin sat the back door of Diamond Tooth Gertie's, the Yukon's most notorious casino. Not only did the walls of my tiny cabin seem to box me in, but late into the night I heard the giggling of dancehall girls who had stepped out the back door of the casino for a smoke. In the distance I could hear the incessant sound of tinkling slot machines and the merriment of barroom piano playing. It was almost unbearable.

One night, Gertie's finally got to me. She sank her diamond tooth into my hide and refused to let go. Within a week I had blown every last cent of my savings.

Then I met two Californians who had cycled from California to Dawson, and I rented my car to them so that they could go to Alaska for a week. It didn't take me long to blow that $250, either.

When the Californians returned, they could see that I was in a real situation. "Get out of town," they warned me. The only problem was that I didn't have any money.

When I asked Father Leo, he told me the church didn't have any money either, so I walked to the welfare office and pleaded with them. After much deliberating, they handed me $40 and two five-gallon tanks of gas. I guess they didn't want me hanging around town all winter, making a nuisance of myself.

I managed to make it as far as Liard Hot Springs with the money and gas they had given me. The hot springs are near the border of British Columbia and the Yukon Territory, and the community is nothing more than a small cluster of buildings that include a couple of motels, a souvenir store, a campground, and a gas station. I only had a quarter tank of gas left and Calgary was still eighteen hours away. So I walked into the gas station, hoping that somebody would have sympathy for my plight.

"Whatcha got to sell?" asked the attendant.

"Excuse me?"

"I said, whatcha got to sell? We don't offer no free rides here."

"I'm not sure if I have anything of value," I replied, momentarily stunned. "I've got a bunch of camping gear in my car."

Then I remembered the gold filling that had been ripped from my tooth a few weeks earlier. "And I've got this," I said, pulling the filling out of my pocket.

The attendant called somebody from the back of the gas station, and out hobbled a wizened little Chinese man. "This is our resident jeweller," said the attendant.

The Chinese fellow plucked a small magnifying glass out of his pocket and held it over my filling. "Thirty-five dollars," he said.

"Thirty-five dollars!" I exclaimed. "That thing cost me fifteen hundred dollars!"

"Thirty-five dollars," the attendant repeated. "Take it or leave it."

I took it, although I realized it wouldn't even get me close to Calgary. At least the attendant was gracious enough to let me use their parking lot to raise more funds. Using a black marker, I wrote *GARAGE SALE* in big, bold letters on a piece of cardboard. I propped the sign beside the highway and laid all my belongings across the parking lot: camp stove, foamie, hiking boots, knapsack, cooler, and my army surplus sleeping bag, among other things. I sat there for about two or three hours and ended up making $250.

The next day I picked up two hitchhikers who gave me another $25 to take them as far as Fort St. John. But my tribulations weren't over yet. While driving through a construction zone near Edmonton I hit a bump; the bearings in my left front wheel were immediately pulverized. By the time I reached Calgary the tire was almost bald, and shortly after I drove into a garage for repairs, it deflated. The timing was uncanny.

That trip happened years ago, and needless to say, I'm still trying to figure out where Mary wants me to go. I've since married a lovely woman with whom I've had two beautiful children, and I'm working as a professional wire artist. I've worked at the local zoo sculpting animals out of wire, and I often teach wire art workshops at schools. I even taught my sister how to do wire art over the phone, and she managed to put herself through university on the income it generated.

With a pair of pliers and some chicken wire, I can now make money wherever I go. Best of all, I know that I'll never have to sell another gold tooth in order to fill my gas tank.

Michael Glintz works as a wire artist in Calgary. Since this incident, he hasn't had to sell any body parts to pay for travel expenses.

Seafood Diet

Did that fish just wink at me?

By Jeremiah Sutherland

A few years ago, when I was working for a company that made obscene amounts of cash from the dot-com boom, I had occasion to visit Japan on business. My colleagues and I needed to discuss various issues with the suppliers of our raw material. The Japanese are very big on hospitality, among other things, and we were told that our hosts would expect us to join them for meals. In the case of one supplier, we were invited to spend the entire weekend at an exclusive resort near Mount Fuji.

Well, therein lies the rub. You have to understand that I'm not really what you'd call an experimental gourmet. I am not one of those people who travel around looking to be thrilled and moved to tears by discovering new ways of cooking crawdads or crab eyes. If you switch from Fancy Feast to Tender Tongues, your cat may not jump in and sta rats, bats, gnats … well, you get the picture. But foremost on my list of things I really can't handle is seafood. Especially if it's raw.

Now, add to this list the fact that I seem to have a "sensitivity" to certain other foods, among them beef, soy, and milk products. (People ask me if I'm lactose intolerant and I tell them that I'm just plain intolerant.) I don't turn blue as my throat closes off or anything like that—just imagine Mount St. Helens going off in your stomach and you'll get a pretty vivid picture of what happens to me.

I really like Japan. I like the culture, the country, and the people. I even like the fact that I don't understand the language or what goes on in Japanese heads—this only heightens the intrigue for me.

But man, give me a pass on the munchies!

My intense dislike of all things seaborne (okay, I do eat the odd clam or mussel, but please, steam them) goes right back to the womb. I came out standin' up and talkin' back and I made no bones about the fact that my New Brunswick *confreres* could take their *piscine* buddies and shove 'em. My father would on occasion bring home a salmon freshly caught in the Bay of Chaleur, and I would turn up my nose at the offering.

What is it that I don't like about seafood? Pretty much everything. The taste, the smell, the texture, the appearance of the flesh ... and the BONES! Nothing puts me off more than trying to chew my food while steering my tongue around tiny, needle-like bones. And heaven help me if one of these spiny little things makes it into my throat. It'll put me off eating for a week.

Not to say that in my early days of innocence, I didn't experiment from time to time. Yep, I remember those long winter nights in New Brunswick when we'd sit down to a feed of smelt. Just split 'em, gut 'em, dredge 'em in flour, and fry 'em up in a bit of lard. Yum, yum. Then at some point I realized that the crunchy texture I enjoyed so much was caused in part by the spines that were left in the fish when they were fried. Bye-bye smelts! And let's not even talk about herring and boiled potatoes.

My disinterest in the *fruits de mer* never seemed a handicap until the last ten or fifteen years, when—along with Toyotas and Toshibas—we in North America became inundated with sushi. Raw fish and cold rice wrapped up in seaweed sounds to me like a starvation diet that even Robinson Crusoe would only try after he'd polished off Friday and every coconut in sight. I was dismayed when friends started inviting me out for lunch or dinner so that we could "enjoy" some Japanese cuisine. I would rather drill my own teeth, and said so on many occasions.

So you can imagine my trepidation when it was proposed that I head off for two weeks of traipsing around the backwaters of Japan, talking to people with a sketchy grasp of English and sampling the local cuisine. Like those intrepid English explorers, however, I bought a Lonely Planet guide, packed a healthy supply of meal replacement bars, and caught the plane to Japan with one of my colleagues.

As my colleague had been dealing with the Japanese for almost twenty years, he had a pretty good grasp of the behaviour expected from Western guests, so I listened very carefully to his words of advice. I fully expected to make lots of mistakes, but I wanted to avoid the obvious ones. Spewing snails onto your lap after discovering that they're still alive when you bite into them would be pretty rude.

One thing I have to say in favour of Japanese food is that it is all beautifully presented. Attention to detail being paramount, everything is presented in pleasing arrangements and colours. It truly is a feast for the eyes, if not for the palate.

Now, here's a brief summary of what I experienced:

Breakfast: As we were spending every second or third day in Tokyo, there were several opportunities to stock up on Western-style food. Our hotel even provided Japanese and Western foods in a breakfast buffet. For the first meal of the day, you could have raw egg in hot rice with a side order of seaweed (the seaweed had been processed so that it looked like carbon paper). You could also have "sticky bean," which is sort of like Rice Krispies Squares, except the colour is brown and the beans are only loosely glued to each other. And, of course, you could have fish.

The Western side of the buffet, thank God Almighty, served eggs, bacon, pancakes, and coffee, coffee, coffee.

The most memorable thing I *didn't* eat for breakfast was a fish, complete with head and tail, that had been formed into the shape of a capital *N*. Its head, including a pair of accusatory eyes, pointed straight into the air. Another colleague who had joined us for the second leg of our trip immediately dug in with chopsticks … oh, my!

In a rare show of mercy, another host provided steak, eggs, and toast. However, owing to the fact that I was in a backwater town called Akita (don't bother to look on a map; you won't find it), the chef's grasp of my kind of food was a little shaky. Each slice of toast had enough butter on it to clog the arteries of several Olympic athletes. The steak and eggs ... well, let's just say that the Japanese define "medium well" as "casually introduced to the frying pan." Nothing is ever overcooked, because thorough cooking is not part of the national mindset. Food is either raw or slightly warmed.

Notwithstanding, I fell upon this stuff and wolfed it down without a second thought. The only downside was that, in spite of my colleagues' professed enjoyment of breakfast fish, they wouldn't let me knock off their portions of steak and eggs.

Lunch: As we were visiting a lot of factories, we ended up eating lunches called Bento boxes. Pickled plums, tofu, unidentifiable fish. I ate a lot of meal replacement bars. The less said about this, the better.

Dinner: When it was just the three of us, we would frequently sneak off to have Western-style food ... expensive and poorly prepared, but what the heck. It was a little piece of home. When being entertained, we were fed shark's fin balls wrapped in raw chicken skin (disgusting and really expensive); cow stomach (it looked like Chicken McNuggets and had the consistency of car tires, which was not improved by cooking it on the frying pan placed in the middle of the table); as well as various raw shellfish and noodle dishes.

Thank heavens that all meals were served with lots of beer. Aside from the relaxing effect several beers have on me, it made a lot of the food easier to swallow.

In between meals: Japan is a big vending machine culture. You can buy anything out of a machine. My favourite was the hot coffee in a can, complete with cream and sugar. In my nutrient-deprived state, I had to keep the metabolism going with sugar and caffeine.

Another popular drink was called Pocari Sweat. Unfortunately, no one was able to answer any of my questions about this product—questions like, "What is a Pocari? Why does it sweat so much? How does one collect the sweat of a Pocari?"

I was glad to see that, as in North America, Starbucks is almost everywhere in Japan. Well, really, that's not quite true. In major cities such as Tokyo and Kyoto, the Coffee Mermaid had tapped her tail on many locations, but the countryside of Japan is surprisingly untouched by Western influences. That included, for example, the fact that the Japanese have never heard of fibre, so vegetables and fruit are scarcer than hen's teeth—you certainly won't find them in any restaurant.

Lest you think I'm whining too much, I should just say that the people of Japan are exceptionally hospitable. When we were stuck at the wrong airport in northern Japan, the airport manager bundled us into his car and drove us a hundred kilometres in a snowstorm so we could meet with our contact at the right location. We arrived early and he insisted on buying us lunch. Granted, part of the manager's motivation was to practise his English on us, but nevertheless, *that's* customer service.

Wakino-san, our host at Mount Fuji, also proved to be a gracious host. He took us to what he called a "textile museum," which I must admit I was looking forward to seeing with all the eagerness I feel before a visit to the proctologist. Instead, I was truly astounded by what I saw. For once, Wakino-san's English had not been equal to the task.

This place was only peripherally about textiles. The fellow who does the work, Kubota-san, has invented his own methods of tie-dyeing silk to achieve one of the most astonishing artistic effects I have ever seen. If I had gone to Japan just to see this museum, it would have been worth the trip.

Of course, every good thing must come to an end. And so it was that after two weeks in Japan, my colleagues and I left for home. Even those with cast-iron guts were starting to crave Western food.

Now, do you remember when I mentioned my trouble with milk products? And soy? Do you know what's in those meal replacement bars? Right. My stomach was in a constant uproar, so I guess the final joke was on me. Maybe it's time to buy some shares in Pepto Bismol. After all, I've been buying enough of their product.

Jeremiah Sutherland misspent his young adulthood working as an engineer. In the last few years he has seen the light and become a singer and writer. Visit his web site for independent musicians at www.bullfrogmusic.com. He prides himself on the fact that he has never eaten sushi.

The Rhein in Flames

When a quiet evening cruise turns out to be the next extreme sport.

By Keith Slater

"Do you like me to make booking for Rhein in flames?" said the letter from our Lahnstein hotel.

I had organized a holiday to the Rhein valley in Germany for thirty friends, and the idea sounded intriguing. According to Frau Krühler, our hostess, it was possible to book a dinner cruise to Bingen, a *son et lumière* (sound-and-light show) with castles lit up and a commentary in several languages.

I knew some of the romantic history of the Rhein, including legends about the Lorelei, maidens who were said to lure sailors onto dangerous shoals. So our group forked out fifty dollars a head for the trip.

So it was, on a warm summer's evening, that we found ourselves assembled at the dockside as the *Prinz Wilhelm* sailed into view. Kapitan Stoll and two officers greeted us, standing stiffly erect as we boarded.

"Probably Prussian," I explained when Ben commented on their rigid stance. I was to find out later just how wrong I was.

The boat cruised upriver, stopping at various ports to pick up passengers. At each one, we heard cries of "Der Prinz Wilhelm!" as lackeys rushed to the dockside carrying rubber tires to hang between dock and hull.

"Nice to see how respectful they are," said Maurice. "You've got us the best boat on the river."

"Pure luck," I replied. "Frau Krühler booked it."

We stopped at places I had read about, including Kamp-Bornhofen and the twin towns of St. Goar and St. Goarshausen, on opposite banks near the statue of the Lorelei maiden. Vineyards thrived along the riverbanks; we made inroads into their products and admired the view.

As the sky darkened, the display began. The Prinz Wilhelm joined a flotilla of about eighty boats floating past the castles along the riverbanks, which glowed with light.

The first hint that all was not perfect appeared when the commentary in various languages began. The officer delivering it seemed to be speaking all of them simultaneously, selecting words from each at random, in a voice that seemed far from steady. None of us could make sense of what he said, but we assumed that we were listening to a re-enactment of pivotal events in the region's history.

After we slammed into an adjacent boat, Kapitan Stoll's sudden appearance confirmed our growing suspicions. Clutching a bottle of excellent Rhenish wine, he bellowed a stream of curses over the port beam. The effect was impressive, but would have been still more spectacular if he had directed them to starboard, where the damaged vessel was located. On the bridge, his complement of four officers sprawled over the navigation table, laughing as they consumed more bottles from their crate.

When it was time to turn the ships around, our journey became a nightmare. At the first small village we reached, the cry of *"Der Prinz Wilhelm!"* was preceded by *"Achtung!"* We watched as a veritable army of rubber tires were flung into service.

We soon discovered why. The "landing" consisted of the boat slamming into the dock, causing the passengers who were lining up to leave to fall to the deck. Gales of laughter erupted from the bridge as stevedores scrambled to grab docking lines, their own cries of fury echoing across the river.

Dinner was served on the return voyage, with the flickering remains of the bonfires on shore to occupy our attention. One waitress, Ingrid, served about two hundred passengers, and she was run off her feet. I ordered a favourite dish, Wiener schnitzel, and waited eagerly for its arrival. Ingrid sped from table to table, carrying about a dozen plates at a time precariously balanced on her arms. But mine never seemed to be one of them. I noticed Maurice, who had ordered chicken, suddenly eating fish. *He must have changed his mind*, I thought. *I didn't see him tell Ingrid.*

The next moment, I saw a plate of Wiener schnitzel, apparently on its way to me, diverted to a well-upholstered, middle-aged German woman sitting three tables away. "Hey, she's getting my schnitzel," I said to my wife.

"Didn't you see what happened?" my wife replied. "Ingrid asked who had ordered schnitzel, and that woman stuck her hand up."

I must have been more affected by the wine than I had realized, because I had watched for half an hour without discovering that simple fact.

From then on, my hand went up every time I heard "*Schnitzel, bitte?*" but there were invariably others, even those previously raised for fish or chicken. Eventually I got fish, and I suppose it wasn't all that bad.

We had just left St. Goarshausen on the return trip when I noticed a French girl.

"She got on at St. Goarshausen," I said. "Why isn't she getting off there?"

"Don't be silly!" replied my wife. Although she was aware of my admiration for young women, especially chic French ones, she figured I had misremembered events.

"Yes, she did! There was a whole group of French people that got on at St. Goarshausen."

We slammed into the dock at Boppard, half an hour later, before I was proven right.

One of the French passengers, not quite as drunk as the rest, realized they had overshot the mark. With their fifty clamouring voices, Kapitan Stoll had no choice but to turn around to disembark them. He caught the staff at St. Goarshausen completely by surprise. As he executed another perfect crash landing, a conservative estimate would place the weight of wood removed from the dock at twenty kilograms, an achievement that aroused delirious shouts of joy from the bridge.

It wasn't until half of the French passengers had disembarked that one of them balked at getting off, on the totally unreasonable grounds that he was being dumped on the wrong side of the river. More jollity rang out from the bridge as the disgruntled Gallic contingent reboarded for the crossing to St. Goar and another crash landing.

We set sail once more. Five minutes had passed before I realized that we had a new problem.

"I think we're going the wrong way!" I said to my wife.

"Don't be silly!" was her automatic response.

"We are! We're heading upriver."

She wouldn't listen, so I decided to check with Kapitan Stoll. My German is quite good, but I couldn't understand a word he was saying when I tried to voice my concern. Between roars of laughter, he insisted on offering me wine.

It took three glasses and ten minutes' conversation before I persuaded him to look at the riverbanks. He finally noticed that we were heading upstream and turned us around, to the hearty guffaws of his crew.

And thus began the dock-slamming sequence again, even though we had no passengers to drop off for the next hour. The Prinz Wilhelm zigzagged to and fro, with cries of *"Achtung!"* ringing loudly from every dock, followed by splintering wood and a steady stream of German curse words.

Then, abruptly, the engine stopped. We noticed this immediately, mainly because the lights were simultaneously extinguished.

"What's happened?" my wife asked.

"Sounds as if the engine's cut out," I said. I have this gift for deductive reasoning.

"Brilliant!" was her scathing reply.

"And that's put the lights out," I added, to confirm the acuity of my intellectual abilities.

That was when she became uneasy, along with the sober members of the hundred or so remaining passengers, who began to express concern.

"It's okay," I reassured them. "The engineer will get us going again."

At that point, it dawned on me that my last glimpse of him had been on the bridge, through the upturned bottom of his bottle. I had the uneasy feeling that he hadn't returned to his post afterward.

My suspicions were confirmed when laughter emerged from the bridge, and out wobbled the engineer. A few seconds later, he fell to the floor. A kindly passenger picked him up from the bottom of the stairs and steered him to the next flight with a hard shove as he giggled with delight.

"We're drifting, aren't we?" my wife asked suddenly.

I looked out of a porthole.

"Yes, we are," I told her, "and we're travelling sideways."

Sure enough, we were sweeping beam-first down the Rhein with no lights showing.

For ten minutes, during which I sobered considerably, we strained our eyes to spot any ships bearing down on us. What we would have done if there had been a ship, I have no idea, but watching it ram us would have been more useful than anything the crew were doing.

Of course, miracles do happen. The engine suddenly roared to life, the lights came on, and the engineer went back to the bridge for a well-earned drink.

In the meantime, poor Ingrid was clearing tables, as well as coping with all the serving. We realized that the rest of the dining room staff were in the bowels of the ship following the example of their senior officers. Our first clue was the sound of a breaking bottle, together with more laughter, which reached us from this new direction. Obviously, they had decided to take part in a celebration that was too good to miss.

But, like all good things, the trip came to an end. We were supposed to be back at our dock by ten-thirty, but it was after four-thirty in the morning when we finally crashed into the dock and got off the boat. Ingrid told us that the ship had to set sail again from Bingen at seven the following morning.

We all hoped the passengers on the next cruise would have as good a time as we'd had.

Keith Slater abandoned his precarious existence as a university professor in 2000 for the security of being a full-time fiction writer. He has written fifteen technical books, twenty plays, six novels and thirty short stories. He is active in theatre, with roughly seventy roles as actor (including one memorable occasion when he tried to insult with impunity a member of the Royal Family who was sitting in the audience) and the same number of stints as a director. He lives in Guelph, Ontario.

Hobos at Large

Hopping freight trains to pursue a con man across Canada leads two young bucks to the Promised Land.

By Lyle Underwood

I met Gus in Toronto through a friend of mine who was a car dealer. The thing that struck me most about him was his uncanny resemblance to a penguin, not to mention the wild and shifty look in his eyes.

It was 1947, and my friend John and I wanted to travel out west to find work. Gus assured us that we could work for our train tickets, so we began helping him round up used cars and load them onto railway flatbeds. After two weeks of gruelling labour the flatbeds were ready to go, and Gus told us the "mixed" train (some freight and some passenger cars) would pick us up at the West Toronto station that Friday evening.

We were there, but could only watch as the train rolled right by us. We had been conned. Gus obviously had no intention of paying for our train tickets.

We only had fourteen dollars between the two of us, but we were angry enough that we decided on the spot to follow that train out west and find Gus. We took our duffle bags to a new housing development in North Toronto that night and stayed in a partially built house to keep warm.

Saturday morning we walked out to the highway and started hitchhiking. Our first ride took us to North Bay; the driver must have felt sorry for us after we told him our story, because when we climbed out of his car he gave us two dollars each. We thanked him, bought something to eat and watched for a train that was rumbling west.

Finally we spotted one with farm machinery lashed to the flatbeds, so we climbed on board and found seats on two new Massey Harris combines. From our high perches, we had an excellent view of the passing countryside.

The next day, the train (a steam engine) stopped for water in a small town. I ran to get myself a drink from a water pump in a nearby park, but by the time I had primed the pump, the train was moving again. I took a quick drink, ran after the train and barely managed to catch the tail end of it. I had to work my way forward to the combines; John wasn't sure if I'd made it, and was very pleased to see me.

The next time we stopped, I ran across the tracks to a bakery, where I bought pop and cookies. I was followed back to the train by a railway policeman. After he heard our stories and saw that our work permits were full of stamps, he smiled broadly and told us that he had never seen us.

"And I hope you get your man," he said as he turned to walk away.

It started to rain heavily later that day, and the combines were not enclosed, so for protection we moved to a boxcar half full of wood. The train stopped again, and it wasn't long before we heard a man slamming doors on some of the boxcars. Suddenly the door of the boxcar we were in slammed shut, too.

We started hollering and hitting the sides of the car with pieces of wood until a railway worker heard us. He opened the door and gave us a stern lecture, telling us the car could have been on a siding for a week. After we explained our situation, he invited us into the caboose, and from Strathcona to Winnipeg he shared his tea and lunch with us.

In Winnipeg, we walked downtown and stayed at a twenty-four-hour coffee shop that night. The next morning we walked out to the highway in the pouring rain and started hitchhiking west again. Our first ride took us to Moosomin, Saskatchewan, but along the way we stopped to help several drivers who were stuck in the mud.

The first contact we made in Moosomin was with a Mountie. It was raining so hard that he took pity on us and told us that we could sleep in the jail cells with the doors open. We gratefully accepted his offer, and spent our first (and last) night behind bars.

The next day we reached Tilley, Alberta, and again asked the local Mountie if we could sleep in his jail cells. He took us to a coffee shop and bought us some hot coffee, and another fellow in there bought us a big sandwich. The Mountie came back later and took us across the main drag to meet someone who had bunk beds in his garage, which is where we stayed that night.

In the morning, the Mountie gave us two dollars each, which we used to buy breakfast at a highway café near Brooks. It was at that restaurant that we saw our first real cowboy, Stetson and all.

The next day we hitchhiked all the way to Drumheller, which is where Gus lived. When we finished telling our story to the local Mountie, he informed us that we were dealing with the biggest crook in the valley. He took us to the local bakery, where we ended up staying that night, and bought us fresh buns and coffee.

The Mountie told us how to get to West Drumheller and tried to call Newcastle, where Gus lived. But Gus wasn't home. The Mountie warned us not to harm him, because the police could easily find us.

The look on Gus's face was priceless when we walked up to his house on Sunday morning, eight days after he had left us in Toronto.

Unfortunately, finding Gus didn't do us any good. He told us he couldn't give us any money because everything was tied up on car lots in Calgary. We were angry, but what could we do? We had been so preoccupied with tracking him down that we hadn't figured out what to do when we found him. So we offered him a few choice words and left. In hindsight, the look of surprise on his face was worth every penny.

We slept at the bakery again that night, and the next day we met a man paving streets in the downtown area. He shared his lunch, handed us two dollars each and gave us a few tips on where to find work.

It was harvest time, and John and I soon found work at a couple of local ranches. The man I worked for said his wife would not let me sleep in the house because they had two teenage daughters. I could eat with the family, but I had to sleep in a trailer. His wife wanted to move to Calgary or Vancouver, but he wasn't interested. She must have kept nagging him, though, because a month after harvest he committed suicide.

After harvest had finished, John and I bought train tickets north to Edmonton, but couldn't find any work. We spent the next couple of weeks hitchhiking around Alberta looking for jobs. At one point we had our duffle bags stolen and had to use the last of our harvest money to buy new clothes and gear. One evening we got stranded between Calgary and Edmonton and spent a chilly night sleeping in a farmer's field with nothing but cardboard and hay bales to shield us from the chill.

We eventually got to Calgary and went to a service station where we washed and shaved so that we would look presentable. We stayed at a cheap hotel, and the next day we panhandled down on Eighth Avenue to buy food. We were completely out of money and had nothing to eat.

Back in southern Ontario I had worked at a meat market, so the next day I dropped in at every downtown meat business. There was a meat strike, so the businesses couldn't get much product, but I was finally hired by Handy Meats.

The manager advanced me enough money to stay at the Arlington Hotel on Second Street. As luck would have it, the hotel shared space with a produce store called Handy Produce; the Chinese-Canadian family listened to my stories and fed me breakfast and lunch every day for the next two weeks until I could pay them back.

I worked at Handy Meats making sausage and hamburger for a year, until eventually I was hired as an apprentice meat cutter, following the manager to a new retail stand. John found a job at Shaw Movers, a Calgary house-moving company. He worked a lot of night shifts, so we couldn't connect very often except on weekends.

It was while working at Handy Meats that I started dating two girls, both of them named Shirley. To avoid confusion, my colleagues named the Shirley who would eventually become my wife "Pat." I hadn't expected to get lassoed by a Calgary girl, but I did. I still wear a signature ring with *Love Pat, Xmas 1948* inscribed inside.

Shirley and I later had five children—four sons and one daughter. John was the best man at our wedding. I worked in retail meats until I retired at the age of sixty-two to take care of my beloved Shirley, who by this time had multiple sclerosis.

For his part, John eventually moved to Edmonton. He worked for the Canadian National Railway for a couple of years, and then trained to become a heavy-duty mechanic. He fell in love with an Edmonton girl, married her, and was later promoted to Chief of Services with the Edmonton Fire Department, a position he recently retired from.

John and I still talk weekly and visit one another several times a year. We are good friends after fifty-seven years, and in some way are still those young hobos, standing at the roadside with our thumbs in the air.

It's funny how some things never change.

Lyle Underwood still lives in Calgary, where he swims regularly and skates with a senior's group. His beloved Shirley passed on in August 2003.

Strange Guest

*Norwegians sure know how to make a guy
feel welcome.*

By Jim Sawatzky

My trip to Norway started during an innocuous conversation with my best friend Joe, who told me that his uncle and aunt lived in Lillehammer, a small city in southern Norway. It was the fall of 1971, many years before Lillehammer grew in size and notoriety through hosting the Olympic Games.

Joe's family, the Noviks, had fled the Nazi occupation of their country, crossing the Atlantic in their small fishing boat and arriving on the Canadian East Coast in the summer of 1940. After a short time on the East Coast, the women left to travel by train across Canada to British Columbia; the men sailed the fishing boat down to the Panama Canal, and then north to meet the women on the West Coast.

Some of the family, however, had stayed behind in Norway.

When Joe found out that I was going to Europe for the summer, he told me that I simply *had* to stop and visit his family in Lillehammer. He gave me an address and phone number and told me that he would write and tell them to expect me.

I left Canada with no particular plans, figuring that I would "somehow" support myself as I travelled through Europe. One could say I was a firm believer that planned activities do not lend themselves to spontaneous discoveries. I didn't even take a jacket with me—I knew that I would find one along the way.

So I hitchhiked from Scotland on through Holland, Denmark, and Sweden to Stockholm, and then over to Norway. When I arrived in Norway's capital city, Oslo, it was late fall and starting to get cool. I still hadn't bought a jacket, so I debated whether I should continue north to visit Joe's family or travel south into warmer climes. I realized, however, that Joe's relatives were waiting for me, and I didn't want to make him look like a fool, so I decided to brave the weather and visit them.

I arrived at Lillehammer in the late afternoon, made my way to a local pub, and used the pay phone to call the family. It seems an arrogant presumption now, but at the time, I just assumed that everyone spoke English. After some initial confusion, a young man who could speak English took the phone. I told him, "I have arrived," and asked if they could come and pick me up.

The young man, accompanied by several others my age, arrived at the pub a few minutes later. He turned out to be the boyfriend of the family's daughter, and the only person who spoke any English whatsoever. I was taken to their home and introduced to the parents, who welcomed me warmly, after which the mother led me upstairs to the room I would stay in.

Seeing as I had arrived to visit them, the family asked if the boyfriend would stick around to translate. I had the distinct impression that he did not find this task onerous.

So it was that I spent several wonderful days at the home of Joe's extended family. They fed and entertained me as though I were one of them. The younger members of the family even took me to various local events, including a movie in a nearby town.

On the third day, we were all sitting around the living room, a bird-hunting expedition having been cancelled, when an animated conversation ensued between the boyfriend and the parents. That's when the boyfriend turned to me and said, "They would like to know who you are and why you are here."

I was stunned. Certainly they knew who I was. I was their nephew Joe's best friend. Hadn't he written to let them know I was coming?

Apparently, this was news to them. They had not heard from Joe in years, and had not seen his family since they had fled the country in 1940.

I left the next day, having decided that it was time to visit southern Europe, where jackets were not necessary. When I arrived back in Canada, I sent the Norwegian Noviks a gift package, but the language barrier made it difficult to stay in touch.

I have travelled in many countries since that time, and have met many hospitable people. Yet I will always remember this family for their willingness to pick up a stranger at the bus station, take him in, feed him, entertain him, and only after three days ask him who he is and why he is there. I try to measure my own actions by theirs. If ever a stranger arrives at my door with the announcement, "I have arrived," he or she will be welcomed into my home with no questions asked.

Jim Sawatzky has served in the Canadian military and the RCMP, and has worked for the Solicitor General of Canada. He is still fond of travelling, having lived twice in the Middle East, most recently with his family. He has travelled extensively in Europe and the Pacific Rim, and calls New Zealand his favourite country.

Kima

The trials and tribulations of a first-time mother in Africa.

By Sharon Fitzsimmons

We were in our mid-twenties, newly married, and on the trip of our lives. It was 1972, and my husband Doug and I had spent two years scrimping and saving so we could quit our jobs and embark on a four-month overland journey from London, England to Nairobi, Kenya. We travelled in Land Rovers and slept in canvas tents. Although the trip was not easy and fun, it was always memorable.

Despite encountering exotic sights and sounds almost every day, we weren't prepared for the day we would first meet Kima. When I close my eyes, I can still see the long tuft of black hair that stuck straight up into a peak, the way her big black eyes sparkled when she laughed, and how her long slender tail curled up and over her back, almost touching her head. You see, Kima was not just any baby girl, she was a baby monkey, and during our time together, she would steal our hearts.

We first laid eyes on Kima as we were driving along a road in Zaire (now the Congo). As we drove by—eight foreigners squished into each Land Rover—the natives held her up to show that she was for sale. At the time, Kima couldn't have been more than a few weeks old, and was so small that she could sit comfortably inside a man's palm. The mother monkey would have stood about a metre tall, so she had already been killed for her meat. Fortunately, Kima's tiny body had probably saved her from a similar fate.

Doug stopped the vehicle so we could get a better look. As soon as I held her and felt how frail she was, I couldn't let her go; she would surely have been thrown to the dogs. Doug pragmatically realized that he would have a very unhappy wife and travelling companion if he refused to take the monkey, so he offered the princely sum of two dollars for her. Apparently pleased with our deal, the local natives quickly handed her over. And that's how we came to be the proud owners, or should we say, first-time adoptive parents, of a completely dependent newborn monkey. We called her Kima, short for *Mukaku-kima*, which means "monkey" in Swahili. We later found out that Kima was a rare breed called the Black Mangabey.

If only we'd known what we were getting ourselves into.

It didn't take long to realize that looking after little Kima was a huge responsibility. Any woman who has experienced the emotional and physical roller coaster of looking after a newborn baby will attest to that. Our most immediate concern was how to feed her. She was young enough to still be nursing, and with her mother gone, she looked a bit malnourished. We bought some canned condensed milk from the market and discovered that if we put some on our fingers, she would lick it off. Later, mashed bananas appeased her growing appetite.

As with any baby, there were round-the-clock feedings, diaper changes, and cuddling time, but Kima was even more dependent. As she would have done with her natural mother, Kima spent every moment of the next four months attached to either my body or Doug's. Even those few seconds of air time when she was being transferred from one to the other would cause poor Kima to panic, scream, and pee all over us. I even had to devise a way to dress in stages, relocating Kima to different parts of my body as the dressing progressed. As tiring as it was to look after such a dependent young animal, I relished my bond with Kima, and was somewhat saddened when she eventually grew old enough to start exploring the world more independently.

By the time we arrived in Kenya several weeks later, Kima was growing quickly and had all her hair, but she was still very clingy. Like any baby, she spent her time sleeping, eating, peeing, and making funny expressions. You couldn't help but laugh just looking at her, with a pink bow in her four-inch tuft of head hair, and a diaper with a hole cut out for her tail. Her many human qualities made it easy to forget that she was an animal. She would wake up in the morning, stretch her arms and yawn. Mind you, she also scratched her tummy and her crotch, but teaching her proper manners was too daunting a task.

The group safari ended in Nairobi, where Doug and I spent a tearful day saying goodbye to all our new friends. At the same time, we knew that we had to make a big decision for ourselves: should we return home to Canada or continue travelling on our own through Africa?

Thirty years ago, Africa was not as well-travelled by foreigners as it is today. The inherent dangers, combined with money shortages, made it look like Canada would be the best choice. But just when we were resigned to returning home, we struck a windfall. Doug was offered a lecturer's position in the Faculty of Computer Science at the University of Johannesburg. We were ecstatic to prolong our trip, and spent a month living in a run-down hotel in Nairobi, waiting for Doug's papers for teaching in South Africa to be approved.

During this time, Kima started to explore. At first, she only dared to venture a few steps from us, and would always run back at the first hint of trouble. I often tucked her into my suspiciously oversized purse at the movies or at fancy restaurants. At one particularly upscale restaurant, I transferred her from my purse to my lap. Our dinner table rule was that she couldn't eat from our plates but she was allowed to have any scraps we put beside our plates. Over the course of dinner, I glanced at the next table and saw our neighbouring diner's eyes open wide in astonishment. All he could see was a hairy black hand reaching up from under my napkin to grope around my plate until it found whatever piece of fruit I had left there. To his surprise, the hand grabbed the fruit and disappeared, only to reappear moments later to grope for the next piece. I felt an explanation was necessary, so I discreetly revealed Kima on my lap. Her pitch-black face and wide black eyes, accented by three ridiculously long whiskers poking straight up above each eye, won him over. The man smiled and went back to his dinner.

We experienced lots of firsts with Kima. In fact, we still have the old super-eight home videos of Kima's first tree. Well, it wasn't a tree so much as a small sapling about a metre high. But for Kima, it was her first major challenge, since she was probably only about twenty centimetres tall at the time. This "tree" was so wiry that Kima's full two kilograms, when perched at the very top of the tree, were enough to bend it all the way to the ground, where she could safely jump off. Once she mastered this tree-climbing exercise, it became her favourite game.

After a month in Nairobi, Doug's papers came through, so we flew to Johannesburg, South Africa. The airline's rules dictated that animals had to be in the cargo area of the plane, but that would have been absolutely traumatic for Kima, who had never been more than a metre away from us. So we smuggled her onto the plane. First we drugged her with a mild tranquilizer that we got from a sympathetic veterinarian at the university in Nairobi. We waited until the last minute to board, hid her inside Doug's jean jacket, and made our way to customs.

Unfortunately, we had overstayed our Kenyan visas and the customs clerk spent several minutes chewing us out. Later, we realized he was trying to get us to pay him, but being the naive Canadians we are, we didn't understand. Meanwhile, we were sweating. Kima was inside Doug's jacket, but her tail was hanging below it, advertising her presence. Luckily, the clerk couldn't see anything below the counter, so he remained oblivious to our travelling companion.

For many long minutes we stood at that counter until one of the flight attendants rushed up to us and asked if we were Doug and Sharon Fitzsimmons. We were the last passengers to board the plane and they were holding it for us. With that, Doug turned to the customs guard and said, "Sorry, but we have to go"; we took off running toward the plane, grinning the whole way.

Once the plane was in the air, we felt that we were safe; Kima came out of hiding and all the flight attendants came over to take a closer look. She was still a bit groggy, but was willing to smile and be cute. It was only after landing in Johannesburg that the pilot came up to us and voiced his displeasure. He was angry that we had smuggled her onto his plane. He was a loud, arrogant man who kept insisting that he would have killed Kima had he known she was on board. The idea of anyone hurting poor Kima made me break into sobs, but apparently that's what he had set out to do, since he left us alone after I started crying.

South Africa had a one-month quarantine requirement for out-of-country monkeys, so Kima was taken from us and put into quarantine. This was to be our most significant separation yet, and I worried terribly about how Kima would fare. As it turned out, I should have been worried about how I would fare, since I seemed to take our separation harder than Kima did. Luckily, the facilities were clean and new. Kima even had a cage to herself. It was only a metre wide, but about three metres high and three metres long—more than enough room for her to jump around in. The workers were very kind and allowed me to visit every day, which was good for both of us. Finally, after about two weeks, the workers cut us some slack and let us take her home early. Or maybe they were just sick of seeing my face pressed against the window every morning, begging to be let inside.

Home for us was an apartment over some stores in a run-down area of Johannesburg, within walking distance of the University of the Witwatersrand. Kima had the run of our apartment and we felt like a family again. Only once did we leave the apartment without her, and we had to hire a babysitter to make sure the house would still be intact by the time we came home. The rest of the time, Kima was our constant companion while we explored our new city, which meant we were always surrounded by curious people.

Even though South Africa has a lot of wild monkeys, it is illegal to own a monkey unless it is from another country. She was adorable, and like any proud first-time mother, I loved all the attention my baby received. By now she didn't want to be in my purse and would sit on Doug's shoulders and hang on to his hair. Kima was becoming more independent, and since we had a steady paycheque from Doug's job, so were we. We decided to use the last of our funds to purchase a Volkswagen Beetle, outfitted for life on the road.

We spent many days in that car, visiting everywhere that lay within a few days' driving distance. Doug's teaching schedule permitted four-day weekends and we made the most of them. Kima took great pleasure in sitting on the top of the back seat, enjoying the view. Every once in a while she got lonely back there and would join us in the front seat. Instead of walking down the seat, however, Kima did what monkeys do—she grabbed a hunk of Doug's hair and swung herself forward. There was never any warning when this might happen, and it added a new dimension of challenge to driving, for Doug would have to keep us on the road while Kima used his hair as a vine.

To avoid this, we tried to come up with ways to keep her occupied. As with every toddler, we found that distracting her with food worked quite well. She especially liked grapes, but she was fussy and wouldn't eat the skins. She didn't mind peeling them herself, but then she would leave the dried-up skins all over the car. To protect our car, I relented and peeled all the grapes before we left home.

Doug had other struggles with Kima. When we weren't travelling, Kima enjoyed sitting on Doug's chest or shoulders, picking through his hair to look for bits of salt or bugs. At fairly regular intervals, certain that she had spotted some intruding insect, Kima would grab a fistful of Doug's hair, yank them out by the roots, and hold them up to her face so close that she would go cross-eyed staring at them. Inevitably, she would realize nothing was there, shake the recently uprooted hair onto the floor, and continue searching. This was certainly a primary cause of Doug's premature balding.

To protect our apartment, I also toilet trained Kima. About every two hours, I would perch her on the toilet seat and command in a singsong voice, "Go pee pee Kima. Go pee pee." This was usually followed by the telltale noises of a good monkey following orders. I have no doubt Kima would have been fully toilet trained, except she couldn't lift her tail out of the toilet water. African monkeys, as opposed to American monkeys, have no control over their tails. So my role became that of tail-holder during Kima's bathroom visits. What a mother doesn't do for her baby!

By then, Kima was an expert climber, and her climbing toys had extended from that first scrawny tree to include Doug and myself, the furniture, and best of all, the family room drapes. One of Kima's favourite games was to dash up the drapes, stand poised on the curtain rod, and then leap off with four legs spread wide. She always seemed visibly thrilled at the ferocious CRASH! she made when she landed on newspapers that were usually strewn on the couch.

The game worked fine until the time "Grandma" came for a visit.

Doug's mom flew from Windsor, Ontario to Johannesburg for a week-long visit. Being a young wife, I was very aware that she seemed to regard me as the woman who had caused Doug to lose his mind, quit his job, and spend years travelling in Africa. Grandma was a very conservative, hard-working woman. Until this visit, her most distant trip had been to move from her prairie homestead in Saskatchewan to Ontario, and she made it clear that she did not approve of the frivolous expenditures Doug and I were making on this trip.

In addition, she was highly suspicious about keeping a wild monkey in the apartment. I was determined to spend the week proving that I was a good wife, and that travelling to Africa wasn't nearly as scary as Grandma assumed. So it was much to my chagrin that I found Grandma napping on the couch one afternoon with the newspaper lightly folded across her chest.

I immediately took stock of the situation, scanning the room to find Kima. Sure enough, she was exactly where I'd hoped she wouldn't be—hanging off the drapes. Kima and I locked eyes, and by the excited gleam on her face, I knew exactly what she had in mind. I lunged for Kima, but she was too quick, playfully dodging my attempt to stop the inevitable. There she sat on the curtain rod, carefully analyzing the best angle from which to leap. I whispered urgently to Kima, explaining why she couldn't—really shouldn't—jump on Grandma. All the while, Kima stood with her legs outstretched and her head angled forward and down like a high-diver, preparing for her most challenging dive yet.

Finally, I decided to get a chair so I could reach Kima. As soon as I turned my back, of course, Kima grabbed the opportunity and made like a flying squirrel. She propelled herself off the drapes with all the power her tiny body could muster. She dropped through the air with her little hands flailing, only to land with a satisfying CRASH! squarely on the newspapers laid across my soundly sleeping mother-in-law. Did I say soundly sleeping? Never before had one of Kima's jumps produced a noise quite like the one that erupted from Grandma as she woke to find a writhing ball of monkey scrambling across her. Poor Grandma. It took a few minutes to calm her down, and I doubt she slept much during the rest of her visit. So much for making a good impression!

Kima was almost a year old by the time Doug's contract at the university was complete, and we were again faced with a tough decision. Now that we had replenished our bank account, we decided to head back home to Toronto via South America. But how could we bring Kima along? I spent many hours contacting consulates and permit offices, trying to find a way to keep Kima with us. But most countries didn't allow monkeys, and if caught, she would either be killed or put in quarantine for at least six months.

Given the dismal reports of conditions in human jails in those countries, I didn't even want to consider what the animal quarantines would be like. The chances of getting caught were too great. With our hearts broken, the only option was to find her a new home.

The zoo didn't want her because they knew the other monkeys would reject and probably kill her. It wasn't an option to set Kima free, either. Not only had she been coddled and spoiled for all her young life, but Kima was a North African monkey. She was completely unprepared for the conditions and predators in South Africa.

Eventually, we heard about a family who lived on a farm near Pretoria, just north of Johannesburg. This family was unique because they kept zoo animals instead of farm animals. After hearing our story, they agreed to meet Kima. It didn't take long for them to fall in love with her the same way Doug and I had a year earlier. She was bigger and bolder by now, but loved to be cuddled by anyone who was willing to give her attention. Not surprisingly, they were thrilled to adopt Kima.

Although I was grateful to have found a loving home for her, I was not yet satisfied. There was no way I could give up my baby without doing a thorough background check on the couple who were taking her in. On more than one occasion, Kima and I would pop in unexpectedly, half-hoping to catch them in the act of some evildoing. On one late-night espionage mission, I cautiously tiptoed up to their family room window to peer in and see how they were treating their animals. After several minutes of watching and listening, I tiptoed away again, smiling sheepishly, finally convinced that the family really was as loving as they proclaimed. The mom had been tenderly knitting a sweater for Kima, whose native Zaire was much more tropical than the high country of South Africa.

Despite the loving family we gave her to, I can still feel the pain of giving her up. It was a deep wrench in my gut that, even after thirty-three years, I can feel as I remember her sweet little-girl ways. We brought her to the farm about a month before leaving for South America so we could be sure it was working out. Every few days I would make a surprise visit to see if they were treating her well. But it was obvious they loved her. She was loose on their farm during the day and slept in the house at night. Finally, I was satisfied she would get the attention and love she deserved.

You can perhaps imagine our anguish, then, the day the farm called with some sad news, a few days before Doug and I were to fly to South America. "I'm sorry Sharon, I have some bad news. Kima passed on during the night." There was a long pause on the other end of the phone. "We don't know why. She must have picked up some virus that she wasn't accustomed to fending off. We brought her to the zoo veterinarian this morning, but he couldn't do anything to help her. I'm so sorry."

We never saw Kima again.

Little Kima was with us for only a year, but we'll always love and cherish the memories we have of her. Would it have been better not to interfere in the first place? If we hadn't, she wouldn't have survived as long as she did. Of course, we don't know the answer. All we know is that she brought unimaginable love and joy into our lives. We like to think she remembers us as the parents every young monkey should have.

Doug and Sharon Fitzsimmons currently split their time between retirement communities in Guelph, Ontario and Florida. They have two children who are not only potty trained, but are working on Doctorate degrees.

Seal of Approval

Wild encounters in Canada's third-largest city.

By Philip Torrens

I t was a perfect summer evening for paddling on Vancouver's English Bay. And I had the perfect companions: a pair of pretty damsels, Tracie and Susan, on their first kayak outing. Determined to be worthy of their trust in me as escort, I ran them through a complete pre-paddle checklist of safety procedures, including "rafting up"—laying two or more kayaks alongside one another for stability in rough water. Not that we would ever need to raft up on the millpond-smooth surface of the bay that evening.

Or so I thought.

Once we were afloat, the admiration in my charges' eyes encouraged me to begin showboating, quite literally. I ran shamelessly through my repertoire of paddling skills. "And this," I explained, nonchalantly leaning my kayak at right angles to the water, "is called a brace." With a long sweep of my paddle I prevented the kayak from capsizing.

I then regaled them with tales of a training exercise for bracing that I'd nicknamed The Amorous Walrus. "My buddies and I take turns straddling the back of each other's boats. We then heave ourselves from side to side, trying to flip the boat over. After a while your bracing gets good enough that nobody can get you over, no matter how hard they try."

We'd been underway for just ten minutes when we encountered one of the rarest of all sea creatures: the social seal. Over many years of kayaking, I've encountered dozens of seals, but never before or since has one behaved as this one did. Typically, seals watch with idle curiosity as you paddle past haul-outs where they sun themselves on the rocks, looking like overfed tourists at a seaside café. If you approach too closely, they will reluctantly stir and ease themselves into the water, staring at you reproachfully as they do so. Sometimes, seals stalk kayakers stealthily from behind—your first inkling of their presence is a startling splash as they up-end and dive. In a few cases, you will become aware of a dark head bobbing in the waves in front of you, a head that will slip beneath the surface as silently as a periscope once its owner realizes you've spotted him.

But Sammy, as we dubbed this particular seal, modelled his behaviour more on Flipper the Dolphin than on Nessie the Loch Ness Monster. He surfaced just a few fathoms beyond our bows, eyed us expectantly as we came closer, and then swam boldly toward the back of Tracie's boat.

He scrabbled at the slippery side for a bit, but with its smooth, glossy finish, the kayak was clearly not designed for receiving flippery boarders. (Imagine trying to scale a plate-glass window while wearing wet fur mitts.) Sammy quickly hit upon the logical solution: a running start. He submerged, and then launched himself like a breaching mini-whale onto Tracie's back deck. By this time

I'd rafted up our kayaks in the approved manner of a veteran, slipping my arm around Tracie's waist—purely to offer stability and reassurance, of course.

Once he was on board, I could estimate Sammy's weight at about fifty pounds, making him a youngster in seal terms; adult seals would tip the scales (and, presumably, the kayaks) at three or more times that. He proved to be as interested in us as we were in him, peering closely at us with his large, limpid eyes. As he breathed down Tracie's neck, she got a bit nervous. I couldn't blame her. For all their cuteness, seals have big, strong teeth, and plenty of them. Seals are essentially wild dogs in diving suits, and dogs can hurt you even with what's intended to be a friendly or exploratory nip. So I tipped Tracie's kayak to about a forty-five degree angle, decanting Sammy smoothly into the sea.

Our curious new friend took no offence at this. Now a practised hand, he launched himself back aboard, this time onto the bow of my boat.

Over the next half hour or so, he boarded and examined all three of our rafted boats, front and back, like a Victorian admiral inspecting his fleet—a resemblance enhanced by his comic-opera moustache and his barks of apparent approval as he found everything shipshape. Every so often, perhaps weary of his seafood diet, he would start gnawing experimentally on the deck lines or fixtures of our boats, and I would have to tip him over the side again. These periodic dunkings all seemed to be part of a grand game as far as he was concerned.

Eventually we had to evict Sammy one last time and start paddling homeward. But Sammy wouldn't take the hint. In his mind, we were merely playing a new and more challenging game: Leap Aboard the *Moving* Kayak. Since we weren't rafted up while paddling, it was fortunate that he selected my boat as a target, because fifty pounds of torpedoing penniped packs quite a punch.

The first time he came rocketing aboard, he caught me unawares. As he crash-landed on my deck, I flashed my paddle out into a brace just in time to avoid capsizing. Again and again Sammy shot out of the sea, skidded across the back of my boat as it canted in response to his impact, and belly-flopped back into the water. If he had been able to shriek in delight, I'm sure he would have. Fortunately for my pride, none of these torpedo-like attacks actually overturned me. But it was frequently a very near thing.

Somewhere near the shore, Sammy disappeared, either tired of the game or made bashful by the human swimmers off the beach. Every time I've paddled those waters since that evening, I've kept an eye out for him, hoping to feel the familiar thump of a passenger dropping in for a visit. But there has been no sign of him. Maturity may have changed Sammy's habits, blending him into anonymity amidst his fellow seals. (And they're as hard to tell apart as monks; I may have passed him a dozen times and never known it.) Or perhaps he has simply swum on to pastures new.

Happy landings, Sammy, wherever you are.

Phillip Torrens works for a major outdoor equipment retailer in Vancouver, where he frequently trades his paycheques for paddling gear. He's glad that this close encounter was with a seal and not an Orca whale.

Dracula's Curse

Brasov can be a spooky place after dark.

By Erica Amery

Eastern Europe has always intrigued me. In particular, Romania—where Count Dracula reputedly lived—has an exotic, untouched allure. I had always wanted to see the mysterious medieval setting I had read about in books and seen in pictures. Little did I know that my visit there would leave me feeling that the Count himself had led me astray.

I had already travelled through parts of Western Europe and was working in Edinburgh when the travel itch flared up again. I ended up on a train to Bucharest with my Aussie flatmate, Penny. We had booked a *couchette*, figuring it would allow us privacy to sleep. We were sadly mistaken; throughout the day, authorities pounded on our door continuously, brusquely asking to see our passports. When we finally reached Bucharest at nine that evening, our objective seemed fairly simple: find a bank machine and a cheap place to stay near the train station.

Our taxi driver, however, turned this simple task into a twenty-minute ordeal that almost tripled the fare we had agreed on. Our hotel clerk later told us that we had been given the "scenic" tour of Bucharest and that the train station was only a ten-minute walk away.

The next morning we caught our train to Brasov, the gateway to Transylvania and the land of Dracula. As we stepped off the train, a short, stocky man greeted us with a friendly smile and open arms. He looked to be in his mid-thirties and introduced himself as Yousef. He was offering a vacant room at his mother's home that would comfortably sleep two.

Penny and I were wary of getting ripped off again, but we didn't want to spend the rest of the day looking for cheap accommodation. We decided to take a chance and piled into Yousef's old Volvo. After a bumpy twenty-minute ride through narrow cobblestone streets, we pulled up to a small, whitewashed stone bungalow with a faded red roof. Yousef described the place as perfect for our needs.

"It's only a fifteen-minute walk to the city centre," he assured us, showing us a panoramic view of the city from his mother's porch. As we admired the view, the door swung open and a small plump woman with a head of silver hair peered at us timidly. Maria looked like a miniature version of her son, Yousef. She did not speak any English, but she would be happy to rent the room—a small suite with a double bed, bathroom, and an old black and white TV. We agreed on a price, and then hauled our bags out of the Volvo and dumped them on the bed. At last it was time to explore the town; we grabbed our wallets, camera, and trusty guidebook, and set out on foot.

As Yousef had promised, the walk to the *piata sfatului* (the city square) was only fifteen minutes. We explored the city's spectacular gothic architecture by way of a self-guided walking tour, as recommended by the tourist bureau. The highlights included the Black Church, its dull black walls scarred by the Great Fire of 1689, and the *Poarta Schei*, the original city gate with its four captivating towers. Our explorations culminated in an extravagant Romanian meal of *muschi de vaca* (small cutlets of veal), salad, and brioche for dessert, all washed down with a bottle of delicious Romanian wine.

While we easily could have stayed and had another bottle, we decided to call it a night. We were leaving for Bran the following morning, where Dracula's infamous castle awaited us, and we wanted to get an early start. As we strolled back to our neighbourhood, giddy from the wine, we talked excitedly about the day's events, the people we had met, and our plans for the following day. Caught up in conversation, it took us quite a while to realize that we had passed the same corner store, the same row of houses, and the same school—three times. We had been walking around in circles!

We quickly discovered that we were missing one small but very valuable piece of information: the name of our street. We knew what the house looked like, we had the street number, but we had forgotten to check the street name.

For the next couple of hours, we trudged up and down the streets, trying to spot Maria's house. As the sun began to set, we became increasingly worried. The town really did look quite gothic and mysterious in the dark. Fittingly, we could hear howling in the distance, surely vampires and werewolves stalking the streets of Brasov for unsuspecting "tourist fare." When we heard footsteps behind us, terrifying thoughts raced through my head.

"Are you girls all right?" asked a friendly voice with a thick Romanian accent. We turned to see a tall, thin man with a mass of curly black hair hanging over his eyes. "My name is Marius. Can I help you?" His bright blue eyes and soft voice did not seem like those of a vampire, but rather a guardian angel who might lead us to salvation. Still on edge, we cautiously explained our situation.

Marius noticed our guidebook and asked if he could look at it. He leafed through the accommodation section and stopped at an advertisement that read: *Pensiune: A fifteen-minute walk northeast of the city centre. The owner's son greets travellers at the train station. The owner speaks no English, but the accommodation is clean and she is very friendly.*

"Could this be the place?" asked Marius.

It sounded promising, but we couldn't be sure.

"Follow me," said Marius, taking charge. He led us to his house, where a short plump lady greeted us. Marius explained our situation to his mother and called the number in the ad. We looked at him expectantly, but it was the wrong house. Feeling pathetic, we thanked Marius and his mother and stepped out onto the street, determined to continue the search for our *pensiune*.

Minutes later, Marius caught up to us, crying out that he had thought of a solution. Once again we trusted our new friend and followed him through the winding cobblestone streets to a large cement building with bars on the windows. He opened the door and as we entered, four large men wearing blue uniforms and white caps stared at us suspiciously. Marius had brought us to the local police station.

After Marius explained our situation, the officers' demeanour changed from suspicion to concern and slight amusement. "You are lost. What is your address?" one of the officers asked in broken English. We admitted sheepishly that we only had a description of the house and the number, but no street name. After some chortles and whispers, the police escorted us outside. Rather than turning us away, however, they locked the station door behind them and joined in the search. Now we had Marius and seven officers—an entire detachment of the Romanian police force—helping to solve the mystery of the disappearing *pensiune*.

We split into teams and continued our search. Seconds turned into minutes, and minutes into hours, but the officers stayed with us. After two hours of combing the city for our *pensiune*, two of the police officers walked up to a brightly lit porch to question an elderly couple. From the street we could see the elderly man stand up and point down the hill. The expression on the officers' faces lifted, as though they had found the missing link to crack the case.

"Follow us," the men said confidently. Penny and I followed them down the hill, directly to a little white house with a red-tiled roof. We looked at the number on the house: 64. This was our *pensiune*, the one we had been looking for all evening! Strangely,

Penny and I had searched this street earlier and could have sworn that we had stood in that exact spot. But there hadn't been any trace of an old whitewashed house with a red-tiled roof.

We thanked Marius and the police officers profusely. Before they left, one of the officers opened our guidebook and wrote down the address in big bold letters. "Don't forget to write down the address next time," he said, smiling kindly.

As we approached the house, we were greeted at the door by our hostess. "Good day?" she asked in broken English.

Penny and I exchanged knowing smiles and said, "We're happy to be home." To this day, I wonder if on that night in Brasov, we were caught under the curse of Count Dracula!

Erica Amery has been bitten by the travel bug many times, which she claims is more appealing than being bitten by Dracula. She lives in Calgary when she's not flying off to exotic destinations around the world.

101 Ways to Destroy a Camera

Trade secrets of professional travel photographers.

By Matt Jackson

When I'm feeling mirthful, I sometimes tell people that I became a professional photographer because I dropped my camera off a bridge.

The bridge in question was the suspension bridge that spans Logan Creek Canyon on Canada's famous West Coast Trail. The camera in question was an expensive point-and-shoot number that my beloved grandparents gave me for my twenty-first birthday. This camera, in turn, was a replacement for another point-and-shoot that I had drowned in a river the previous summer, when I inadvertently flipped the canoe I was paddling. Which in turn replaced a camera that I dropped while hiking down a steep mountain slope in 1992; I've never seen a camera bounce quite as high as that one did.

Anyway, back to the West Coast Trail. I made a very noble attempt to save the camera my grandparents had given me as it fell from the bridge. I remember it bouncing from hand to outstretched hand several times—wet and slippery hands, I might add—before careening off a steel cable and over the edge. I remember feeling the organs in my chest tighten as my prized birthday gift fell through empty air, bounced off a large rock, and shattered into several pieces.

The reason this episode relates to my becoming a professional photographer is that, at the time, I had no money. I had spent the winter working weekends and skiing on weekdays. If my bank account were admitted into hospital, I'm sure it would have been hooked up to a life support system. The only camera I could afford was an old Ricoh manual camera that my friend Jason was trying to sell so that he could upgrade. The Ricoh was cumbersome and heavy, but nearly indestructible. It was the kind of camera that if you dropped it on marble flooring, you would get down on your hands and knees to make sure it hadn't cracked the marble.

I think it's important to mention here that I never planned to learn about photography. I really just wanted an easy-to-use, please-no-hassle kind of camera that would record a few memories from my year in western Canada. These memories would remind me of countless adventures, even if the pictures were not perfect. Yet with my new Ricoh, I had no choice but to learn about photography. The camera didn't have a fully automatic function. The only way I would get pictures, it turned out, was if I learned to shoot with it in manual mode.

But this was what got me hooked on photography, so I can't complain. By the time I returned to university in the fall of 1994, the Ricoh had become my constant companion. Moreover, it gave me the perfect excuse to skip class from time to time. There were several occasions when good light would just happen to coincide with Finance class, and I would be obliged to spend the class in a park taking pictures of children playing or fall colors or something like that. These coincidences were really quite remarkable.

A couple of years after I purchased the Ricoh, I graduated from university, which is when I decided to make my official plunge into the uncertain world of professional photojournalism. An uncle loaned me several thousand dollars so I could upgrade my camera gear to professional-calibre equipment. The Ricoh had survived two years at my side, so I was hopeful that my days of destroying cameras were behind me.

I couldn't have been more wrong.

In the spring of 1997, eight months after purchasing my new camera gear, I decided to hike the West Coast Trail again, as well as the newly established Juan de Fuca Marine Trail. My friend Cam and I planned to spend eleven days hiking the trails back to back; little did we know it would be one of the most challenging trips we would ever do. Over eleven days, we endured ten days of rain, and watched the trail become a gigantic mud slick.

Cam's camera—or rather, his girlfriend's camera—was the first casualty. On Day Three, while fording the mouth of Loss Creek, Cam got stranded in the middle between pounding surf and flooding river. The current was so powerful that it defied him to get to the far side. For many minutes he just stood in the river with a pained look on his face, wondering what to do next. Eventually he realized that he had to move, so he lurched forward step by step and somehow managed to reach the far bank without toppling over. What he didn't realize was that his erratic lurching had dislodged his girlfriend's camera, which was by that time on its merry way to Japan.

The casualties continued. On Day Eight, during a break in the weather, we found ourselves hiking along a sandstone tidal shelf at low tide. There were dozens of tidal pools full of starfish, purple urchins, and turquoise anemones, and just offshore were several dozen barking sea lions congregated on a large haul-out rock. I brought out my camera and tripod to take pictures of some starfish in one of the tidal pools, but turned momentarily to grab something out of my camera bag. When I turned back, it was just in time to watch my camera perform a perfect Greg Louganis nosedive into the water.

Fast reflexes on my part, combined with the fact that it was a shallow tide pool, saved the camera. However, the unprotected lens smashed hard against a rock at the bottom of the pool.

I wish that I could say I was gracious and philosophical about losing a practically new $2,500 camera lens, but that would be an exaggeration. Actually, it would be a downright lie. After I finished berating the starfish for not making even a feeble attempt to save my falling camera lens from certain death, I turned my seething anger on the sea lions. Judging by their boisterous revelry, they were having some laughs at my expense.

It was about this time that Cam decided it would be in his best interests to hike ahead for a while and leave me to my ranting. By the time we met up an hour later, I had calmed down sufficiently to once again engage in conversation not laced with profanity.

Over the course of that summer, I also managed to sacrifice several expensive tripods—which, I assure you, requires a great deal of practice, dedication, and effort. Tripod Number One I left at a public hot spring, and when I returned to retrieve it twenty minutes later, it was gone. Tripod Number Two met its timely demise when a friend of mine was loading my backpack into his car. The tripod was strapped to the side of my backpack, and as he hoisted it in, one of the legs caught on the roof rack and snapped off.

My favourite story, however, relates to the death of Tripod Number Three. I was in Vancouver at the time, and riding the public transit system with my large backpack in tow. This proved to be rather awkward, because many of the buses have folding doors with a metal bar running down the middle of the doorway. Trying to squeeze oneself through half a door while hefting a monstrous backpack is—how can I put it—defying the laws of physics?

It was on one such bus, while trying to exit through the back door, that a leg of my tripod caught on something. After much struggling, I managed to get loose by rotating my body sideways. This resulted in one of the tripod legs sliding out of its metal clamp, bouncing down the stairs, and rolling under the rear wheel of the bus. Before I could retrieve it, the bus driver hit the accelerator and effectively turned the tripod leg into tinfoil.

The summer of 1997 was a costly one, with a cumulative loss of more than $3,000 worth of camera equipment. Even so, it still doesn't compare with my greatest performance. By 2002 I had graduated into the ranks of professional travel photographers, so I was far better prepared to execute (and subsequently deal with) one of the most spectacular camera-destroying events in the history of mankind.

As chance would have it, this episode also happened while I was hiking with Cam, who had witnessed my novice efforts at camera annihilation five years earlier. This time, we were hiking along a high ridge near Waterton Lakes National Park in southern Alberta. It was our last day of a five-day backpacking trip through the high country, and we had just arrived at the end of a long ridge from which we had to descend.

The brochure we'd consulted had assured us this would be quite straightforward, but looking back on it, I realize that the brochure had probably been edited by mountain goats.

A steep cliff blocked our descent route, but we were eager to get home, so we decided to try lowering our backpacks with a rope and then down-climbing free from the extra weight. We had both done this before in similar circumstances. Preparing to tie the rope to my backpack, I leaned it against a rock beside the precipice. I made a loop in the rope, and as I leaned over to tie it to my backpack, the pack fell over (translation: jumped sideways) and dropped over the edge.

For the next minute or more, Cam and I watched in horror as it bounced, somersaulted, and otherwise careened out of control down a 2,000-foot mountain face. The backpack split down the middle and its contents—which included a camera, three lenses, a tripod, film, and various camera accessories—exploded across the rock.

The backpack eventually reached the bottom of the cliff and stopped, by this time emptied of its contents. Cam and I stood silently for what seemed an eternity. Perhaps Cam expected an explosion like the one he had witnessed on the West Coast Trail. But I am pleased to report that I had evolved beyond such childish tantrums. With great courage, I turned to Cam and said, "Well, I guess we shouldn't go down that way."

I hold to this day that a person hasn't really lived until he or she has watched $7,000 worth of uninsured camera equipment bounce down a mountain face.

If that is the case, I know other photographers who have lived equally fulfilling lives. My friend Andrew Mills once watched his $5,000 Nikon swan dive into Emperor Falls along BC's Mount Robson trail.

And then there's the acquaintance of mine—a man who prefers to remain unnamed—who took his $1,500 Hasselblad skydiving with him in the 1970s. After he had jumped from the plane, he was apparently preoccupied with other things. He forgot that he was holding his camera and let go of it.

Another friend, Daryl Benson, was photographing sunset at Vancouver Island's Long Beach when he set his waterproof camera case beside some driftwood so that he wouldn't have to lug it every step of the way. Captivated by the dramatic sunset falling over the Pacific, he allowed his attention to wander. He turned around just in time to watch the rising tide envelop his waterproof case.

From this, he learned an important lesson: A waterproof case is only waterproof when it's closed. None of his equipment survived.

Pat Morrow, the famous Canadian photojournalist who climbed Mount Everest in 1982, once enjoyed an eventful day in the Yukon.

He and two friends pitched their tent near a pass and then climbed a peak in the St. Elias range. They brought their sleeping bags and slept at the summit so Pat could photograph sunset and sunrise.

The next morning, Pat was preparing to fasten his wide-angle lens to his camera when he accidentally dropped it. One of his friends stuck her foot out to cushion the fall, but accidentally punted it over the edge. Pat, ever the gentleman, assured her that it wasn't a huge loss.

When they reached their tent two hours later, they discovered the round, furry backside of a grizzly framed in the tent's doorway. The bear had been chewing on something, and they soon discovered what it was: Pat's 500-millimetre telephoto lens. Fortunately, he was able to repair that one.

In the years to come, I hope to invent many other ways to creatively destroy camera equipment. Then again, maybe not. Although I tell of my trials and tribulations with a dash of pride (what else can I do?), perhaps it's time to move forward and develop another important skill. I call it, "How to Convince Friends to Loan Me Their Camera Gear."

Matt Jackson is president of Summit Studios. He has written more than one hundred magazine articles and is the author of the award-winning book, The Canada Chronicles: A Four-Year Hitchhiking Odyssey. *He recently drowned a $500 camera flash during a month-long paddling trip down Ontario's Missinaibi River.*

Love in the Air

What happens when you get between a lovesick rhino and the object of his affections?

By Lucia Martin

I met my husband Tim while working at a Club Med resort in the Bahamas, so you might say that our relationship was steeped in travel right from the beginning.

I think it was Tim's sense of adventure, coupled with his ability to make me laugh, that proved an irresistible combination. In every group, he was the comedian. The fact that he was able to steal a bus with no brakes and drive it across the island to retrieve dinnerware for some resort guests only hooked me the more. It was simply logical that we should end up getting married.

Our courtship was a long one—five years. Before getting too serious, we decided to test our staying power, and embarked on an ambitious six-month road trip that traced a circle around North America. We started in Ontario and drove across Canada to Vancouver, then down the Oregon and California coasts to Mexico. Eventually we drove across the southern States to Florida and back up to Canada. We set a budget of fifty dollars a day, and basically lived out of our little Honda hatchback.

On the west coast portion of our trip, we walked through Oregon's Pacific surf, explored San Francisco, and camped under the giant Redwoods in northern California. Nothing, however, prepared us for our visit to the San Diego Zoo.

The San Diego Zoo is one of the most famous in the United States, and for good reason. It has a fine selection of animals from around the world, and its "open concept" allows visitors to feel like they are walking amongst the beasties, taking part in their exotic lives. There are no metal bars at this zoo. Rather, deep concrete gullies five to six metres wide keep the residents separate from the visitors. For an animal lover like me, being so close to the animals was a dream come true.

Tim and I spent the morning wandering around, feeling like we were on an African safari. Then, after lunch, we noticed a great deal of commotion coming from the rhinoceros paddock. The male rhino was kicking up quite a fuss, snorting and pawing at the ground with his huge rhino feet. Directly beside him, sitting nonchalantly in the next enclosure, was the object of his deep-seated affection: the resident female rhinoceros. We later learned that she was in heat. Love was in the air, and apparently, it wasn't just Tim and me.

Intrigued, we gathered around to watch the poor rhino perform his mating dance. He seemed to be growing more and more frustrated—and who could blame him? He couldn't reach his mate.

As the minutes ticked by, more visitors arrived to investigate the commotion, and soon there was a large crowd gathered beside the paddock.

And that's when the dam burst, so to speak.

Without warning, the lovesick rhino reared up on his hind legs, his pent-up affections erupting suddenly and catastrophically from his midsection. The confused crowd let out a panicked scream and parted like the Red Sea. Or a rogue wave breaking across a rocky peninsula. Unfortunately, I was the rocky peninsula, and took the brunt of the male rhino's sexual frustration. It was as though somebody had thrown a bucket of milk across my chest.

As for the reaction of my supportive soon-to-be husband, he could barely contain himself. I've rarely seen him laugh so hard. Most of the crowd looked as horrified as I was, but Tim felt no such inhibitions. I excused myself to the ladies' washroom, where I sobbed and did my best to clean up. It wasn't an easy task.

A couple of days later we were visiting friends in La Hoya, a suburb just north of San Diego, when the subject of amorous rhinos came up unexpectedly.

"You'll never believe what I heard today," chortled our friend Bryant. "I'm not sure whether to believe it or not." He went on to describe in painful detail the events of that dreadful afternoon.

Tim and I could hardly believe our ears. "Who on earth told you that story?" laughed Tim. "Lucia was the one who got it."

Now it was our friend's turn to look stunned. "You're kidding!" he said. When he could see that we were serious, he just added blankly, "It was my secretary. She was at the zoo on the weekend."

And then my darling husband-to-be and our good friend Bryant had another belly-busting laugh over the experience. I guess that's what you get when you marry a comedian.

Tim and Lucia Martin live in Kelowna, British Columbia with their three children. Lucia still has an affinity for animals, even rhinos.

Mount Everglades

A climbing trip to Florida's most challenging mountain range.

By Wayne Van Sickle

I grew up near Toronto, Canada's largest city. Unlike many Canadian kids, I had absolutely no childhood experience with camping.

In my late teens, I decided I wanted to learn about wilderness camping, and to travel outside of Canada. So in December of my twenty-first year, I bought a Jeep and began mapping out a serious road trip. I planned to drive southwest to San Francisco and then straight north all the way to Alaska. I figured on leaving in early May and spending the bulk of three and a half months hiking and climbing mountains in Alaska.

I invested a lot of time researching the equipment I would need for the backpacking, hiking, and climbing I planned to undertake that summer. By January, I had purchased it all. As someone with a complete lack of outdoor experience, however, I reckoned it might be smart to try out the gear before I left for Alaska.

At the time, I was employed as a child and youth worker. I worked with a variety of children, including those with troubled histories of family abuse, difficulties with the law, and even severe medical conditions such as autism. Working in this field for any amount of time requires a high level of energy, along with an ability to manage stress and intense emotions. I was good at what I did, partly because I maintained balance in my life. My supervisor, knowing how important my time off was to me, would often make up monthly schedules in which I would work many long days in a row, followed by lengthy stretches of time off. This worked beautifully, because it allowed me to get away and recharge my batteries.

If there was one flaw in this otherwise dreamy scheduling process, it was that I often did not receive my work schedule more than a day or two prior to the first of the month. As a result, I would routinely find myself with long stretches of time off, but virtually no time to properly plan a trip, research a destination, or find a travelling partner. I owe many great misadventures to that supervisor and her scheduling process.

That very winter, for instance, she presented me with my April schedule on the twenty-eighth of March. The schedule was a thing of beauty. I would work two long shifts on the first and second days of the month before taking twelve straight days off. This was the opportunity I had been waiting for! I would have a sufficient amount of time to test my sleeping bag, tent, camp stove, and all the rest of my new camping equipment.

There was only one decision to make: where should I go? The compass may provide 360 possible vectors of departure, but when you live in Canada, and it's April, and all you have is a lightweight tent, there is really only one logical direction to go: south.

So I pulled out my trusty Rand McNally road atlas and pored over the maps of the southeastern US. The fact was, I didn't really care where I went; the specific geographic and cultural qualities of the destination were unimportant to me. All I needed was somewhere far enough south to be warm, and a somewhat mountainous setting where I could start practising for the bigger mountains in Alaska. I wasn't picky.

With only two days before my departure, I didn't have time to dilly-dally, either. I had to buy camping fuel for my new stove, plan a menu, and pack all my gear—all while working two fourteen-hour shifts. I didn't have time to indulge myself in frivolous details, such as looking at the map too closely.

Of course, I knew that in Canada, most of our great mountains are found in protected areas such as national parks. Figuring a similar pattern existed in the States, I scanned the map for the great green blotches that indicate national parks. One quick glance at the metre-high snowdrifts outside my window was enough to convince me that the further south I went, the better.

And so my finger slid down the map in a southerly direction, coming to rest on top of the southernmost national park in the southeastern US: a handsome-looking patch of green called Everglades National Park.

I'm not sure why, but I thought I'd find mountains there.

Perhaps I made a connection between the lexical similarities of EVERglades and EVERest, the world's highest mountain—I'm not really sure. I had been to Florida before, three times in fact, and I probably should have noticed the profound lack of mountain ranges. But these prior visits had taken place during spring break festivities at Daytona Beach and Fort Lauderdale. Cheap beer and the constant parade of Class One bikinis kept my gaze firmly fixed at a low elevation. Apparently, I never once looked off to the horizon.

At any rate, I chose my destination based on this assumption. And with only two days to prepare, I had no time to spend reviewing it. I put in my time at work and plowed on through the preparations. I called my parents and a few close friends to tell them about my exciting plans. None of them were home, so I left messages on their answering machines that I had gone south to the Everglades for a ten-day mountaineering trip.

The amazing thing is, no one called me back to set me straight before I left town. I only found out later that it is a well-known fact, even among Canadians, that the Everglades are not a mountain range, but rather a smelly swamp overrun with big-toothed alligators.

When I pulled up to the US border at Niagara Falls, the border guard smiled at me and asked what business brought me to the United States. I smiled back at the nice man and replied that I was headed south to the Florida Everglades to do a bit of camping and mountaineering. He tilted his head sideways, squinted his eyes, leaned out of his kiosk and asked me if I was gainfully employed in my own country. In fact, he seemed very interested in me, and asked a lot of questions. He wanted to know if I had sufficient finances to support myself, and when my employer expected me back at work. It seemed like a lot of questions. In the end, he waved me through after I showed him a copy of my latest pay stub.

It's a long drive from Toronto to the southern tip of Florida—more than thirty hours of interstate. I passed through New York and Pennsylvania like a bullet on Route 79. Then came West Virginia, Virginia, North Carolina, and South Carolina. I felt like a character in a Bob Dylan song.

In fact, I once saw Bob Dylan in concert. He came out on stage by himself, sat down in a chair, mumbled a lot, and didn't stand up once for hours.

By the time I reached Georgia, I felt I had a lot in common with Bob Dylan.

It had been dark for hours by the time I arrived in southern Florida. I pulled over for the night within a few kilometres of the boundary to Everglades National Park. I was completely wiped out and ready for sleep. Nevertheless, the anticipation of seeing the morning sun rising over the mountains prevented me from falling asleep right away.

I can't say I remember the exact moment, or even the manner in which I learned the true nature of the Everglades. I suspect I have blocked it out of my conscious memory. But at any rate, after a very short time in the park the next morning, I didn't need to consult with a park ranger to confirm that I wasn't going to find any mountains in the vicinity.

If I had visited the park on any other day, with any other expectation, I am sure I would have found the setting exotic and the reptilian population fascinating. I am by character interested in all places new. But on that particular day in April 1993, having come as far as I had with the intention of training for camping in the mountains, I felt a complete lack of wonder. I participated in a very short guided walk around a pond, during which I snapped one picture and did not talk to a single person for fear of revealing where I was from and why I had come so far by myself. Afterwards, I promptly got back into my Jeep, drove through the north gates and took a long nap.

When I awoke some hours later, I got out of the Jeep, looked far off into the distance, and confronted myself with the serious flatness of the Great State of Florida. It was time to come up with Plan B.

I must admit that the whole experience had taken quite a bit out of me. I decided to scrap the training mission for the mountains. In fact, I resolved to abandon all plans for new experiences. I had enjoyed visiting Florida years before, so I decided to simply replicate what had worked in the past. I set my sights on spending a week lying on the beach, drinking cheap beer, and watching all the bikini-clad girls drift by.

In a parallel that I didn't recognize at the time, I once again found myself in the position of having made a hasty decision regarding the goal of my trip, without taking the time to research a specific destination. The tragic misunderstanding of the true nature of the Everglades had not dampened my ability to be decisive. Thus I focused my attentions on what seemed at the time to be a very minor decision: which beach to visit.

Unaware that I was repeating a faulty process, I flipped open my Rand McNally road atlas and scanned the coastlines. Perhaps I had shown a temporary lapse of judgment in placing a mountain range on the map where one didn't exist, but I knew damn well that there were beaches in every coastal city in Florida. Not only that, I knew each and every one of them was superior to any beach in Canada, especially in April.

I used to watch Miami Vice on TV when I was a kid, so I decided against Miami because of the danger factor, and I had already been to Fort Lauderdale and Daytona Beach. The Florida Keys, however, looked appealing. Someone certainly must have had fun naming the various keys: Sugar Loaf Key, Boot Key, No Name Key, even Perky. How could I go wrong? Besides, if Key Largo was good enough to inspire a Beach Boys song, and Key West was good enough for Hemingway, who was I to argue?

Just like that, I started up the Jeep and drove south toward the Overseas Highway, which the atlas informed me was one of the longest over-water roads in the world.

Later that day, I pulled into the KOA campground on Fiesta Key, set up my tent, and changed into my swimsuit. To say the trip to this point had been a disappointment would be an understatement, but I had finally made peace with the fact that I wouldn't be hiking anywhere near a mountain on this trip. Or trying out most of my camping equipment. My angst was slowly being replaced by contentment as I imagined myself sprawled out like a lizard in the sun, toes curled into warm sand. I wandered down to the ocean to stake out a prime place on the beach. It was a little late in the day, but I hoped to find a nice spot.

At the end of the short walk to the ocean, I stopped to take in the scene. There were plenty of people enjoying the sun, even some attractive women. But there was no beach! How about that? In fact, there was not a single grain of sand in sight. The shoreline was composed entirely of jagged rocks. Everyone present had reclining sun chairs to protect them from the sharp rocks of the coastline, but I didn't have one. So I asked one of these sun worshippers the way to the nearest beach. She informed me that the geography of the Florida Keys is such that there is not a single beach anywhere on the keys—the coastline is entirely composed of rocks and coral! And I didn't even have sandals to protect my feet.

Lots of people think Florida is boring, but personally, I find no end to its surprises.

The next day I drove down to Key West, the southernmost tip of Florida. Each evening, the community hosts a quaint little sunset festival on the wharf at the termination of Highway 1. Musicians and street performers provide entertainment as the sun slowly disappears into the ocean. From that point it is only 150 kilometres to Cuba (I've been told they have beaches there).

I arrived back at the KOA campground on Fiesta Key to find the wind picking up. In fact, it picked up so much over the next few hours that I woke up at three a.m., threw my partially dismantled tent into the back of my Jeep, and slept in the driver's seat.

A campground official knocked on the window of the Jeep early the next morning and informed me there would be an emergency meeting in the Games Hall. The wind had indeed been strong during the night. The first thing I noticed upon hopping out of the Jeep was a large and heavy tree branch on the ground. Chillingly, it had dropped in the exact spot where my head had been the previous night … before I moved to the Jeep.

At least I had made one good decision on this trip.

At the meeting, I learned that a sizable storm—one that had not been forecast—was fast approaching from offshore. It would surely be severe, perhaps the magnitude of a hurricane. Officials told us that we should stay put, and that the large, multi-use facility building would be made available for us to sleep in until the storm passed.

I was in a foreign country that was proving to be more foreign at every turn. Although I wasn't feeling too sure of my effectiveness at predicting the local geography, the day and a half I had spent on the Keys told me that being on Fiesta Key during a hurricane would not be a good idea. A narrow highway snakes through the thin key, and the open Atlantic Ocean is never far from the road; the shore often lies only a few hundred metres from the pavement. The Gulf of Mexico is equally close on the other side. There was no damn way I was going to stay on this slim matchstick of land in the middle of the ocean with a hurricane fast approaching. I immediately climbed into my Jeep and started driving north up the Overseas Highway.

The winds were strong, and as I drove, my box-like Jeep was blown like a kite from one lane to another. It was a stressful drive, but I felt a little safer when I reached the mainland and the Keys were behind me. The storm was a big one and there was every reason not to stop, so I continued my journey northward. The winds remained strong and soon heavy rain started to fall. It didn't so much fall as beat its angry fists against the asphalt. The driving demanded intense concentration.

I was weary by the time I arrived in northern Florida, so I decided to stop and look for a hotel for the night. But the tourists were all on the move. A mass exodus northward was underway, and each and every hotel I stopped at was full. It seemed I wasn't the only one uncomfortable with the official directive to stay put and wait it out. As I pressed on, the rain fell more heavily than ever and the temperature began to plummet.

I had driven thirty hours to Florida, but as the old adage goes, you can never really escape the place you are from. I had come to Florida expecting to see mountains and beaches. I could never have anticipated what I saw next: snow.

That's right. Snow was falling from the Florida sky, and it wasn't melting. It began to pile up on the interstate.

Lots of people think Florida is boring, but personally, I find no end to its surprises.

Things didn't get any better as I crossed the state line into peach country. The snow in Georgia was falling even more heavily, and it was swirling about in the wind, making driving dangerous. This was a real Canadian whiteout. I forgot where I was. Thinking I was in Canada, I started muttering to myself in French. The snow was coming down so thick and the winds were so strong that the road was not visible for moments at a time.

Americans were pulling off the road in droves, which deeply offended my Canadian sensibilities. I was worried I might rear-end one of the parked cars. Every good Canadian knows what to do in a whiteout, when the snow is swirling so violently you can't see a metre in front of you: grit your teeth, grip the steering wheel tightly, and hope the road doesn't make any sharp turns before it comes back into sight.

After several periods of whiteout, and after passing even more hotels filled to capacity, I made a crucial decision: I would make a run for Atlanta.

My uncle had married a Southern belle from Georgia. She had moved to Canada, but her parents still lived in Atlanta. I had met them once, years before at the wedding, and they had seemed like nice folks. So I phoned them up with the intention of inviting myself over to their place until the storm had passed.

They were delighted to hear from me, and Southern hospitality being what it is, they invited me to stay with them before I could invite myself. But they had been watching the weather on TV and told me that they doubted I would make it. Apparently I was still a long drive away, and the snow had shut down the interstate and all the major routes in and around Atlanta. It didn't look good.

Still, I knew I would be permanently disowned by each and every one of my fellow Canadians if I allowed myself to be stopped by a snowstorm in Georgia, so I pressed onward. I was determined to make it to Atlanta.

Then the authorities began to take action. State troopers were stopping all vehicles on the interstate to recommend that drivers take shelter for the night. But I still pressed onward.

A while later I came to a roadblock. A trooper informed me that the interstate had been closed due to snow, and that I would need to turn around. I looked him squarely in the eye and said, "It's okay, sir. I am Canadian. I have a four-wheel-drive vehicle. These are normal driving conditions for me. I can make it through, no problem."

In a scene strangely reminiscent of the one in Star Wars when Ben Kenobi and Luke Skywalker are stopped by the storm troopers on their way into Mos Eisley spaceport, the trooper turned to his partner and repeated my words almost verbatim: "It's okay, he's Canadian and has a four-wheel-drive. We don't have to stop him. Let him through."

As his partner moved the roadblock aside, he motioned me over. I pulled up next to him, rolled down the window, and we chatted for a minute about the storm. I recounted that I had left the Florida Keys that very morning and was headed to Atlanta to wait out the storm with my relatives.

I admitted to no fear of the snow conditions, but did mention I was getting tired. The trooper reached into his pocket and held out a hand to me. In his palm were several small, multicoloured capsules. He said, "Well, son, if you know how to drive in this stuff, then your biggest challenge will be staying awake. Go ahead, take these."

Lots of people think the Deep South is boring, but, once again, I find no end to its surprises. There may not be any mountains in Florida, and a total lack of beaches in the Keys. But Georgia has snow, and its policemen give out complimentary "adrenaline" pills.

The snow got deeper and my eyes opened wider. By the time I arrived at my relatives' house I was shaking from the combined effects of the pills and all the coffee I had drunk beforehand.

The city of Atlanta had been brought to a standstill, and it stayed like that for about three days. There were snowmen on every lawn. It looked just like home, except the snowmen were wearing Atlanta Braves hats instead of those of the Toronto Blue Jays.

I was so wired from the caffeine and the drugs that I didn't sleep for two entire days. This was convenient, because I became the safety consultant for the whole neighbourhood. Virtually no one had ever seen snow before, let alone driven in it. People were getting into accidents at every turn. Even the military were unsure of what to do; they were trying to melt the snow by spraying tanker trucks of hot water on it. This made for great ice hockey conditions, but it wasn't so great for drivers.

Suffice it to say that the city of Atlanta needed some advice from a Canadian. My aunt's parents called all the local TV and radio stations to let them know that a Canadian was in the city, and that I could explain to everyone how to drive safely on the snow.

I was busy for the next three or four days helping our Southern neighbours until the snow finally melted. Then it was time for me to migrate home to Canada, the other Great White North.

Wayne Van Sickle has muddled his way through more than twenty countries worldwide. He is the author of two best-selling guidebooks to Algonquin Provincial Park in Ontario, Canada, which he claims to know better than the mountain ranges of southern Florida. You can reach him at stonecut@hotmail.com.

Old McDonald Had a Bike

Our author gears up for a Cambodian transit adventure.

By Conor Grennan

There are two good reasons to bike around the world, and one good reason not to. The first is that before you leave any particular town—for example, Phnom Penh in Cambodia—people will look at you like you're nuts. They'll look at you like operating a bicycle is something they could never possibly do in their lives, or as if you'd just told them you were going to ride to the next town on a chicken or something. It is a really easy way to impress people.

The second reason to ride a bike is that when you get to that destination a couple of days behind everybody who took the bus, and you run into those same people, they once again get that stunned look on their faces. Their jaws drop, they turn to their friends, and say something like, "Do you know how these guys got here? Do you have any idea? On a fuckin' chicken!"

Yup, there's a lot of opium in Southeast Asia.

The reason not to ride a bike, of course, has much to do with taking public transport when you're not biking. In this particular case, there was no way I wanted to spend three days biking the 350 kilometres up to Siem Reap to see Angkor Wat, but my options appeared to be pretty limited. The VIP buses had no roof racks and wouldn't take me, and the boat (which took six hours) cost $25 each way. There had to be another option.

And there was. The saving grace is that in Cambodia, and Phnom Penh in particular, everything is possible. If you have a problem you can't solve, all you have to do is flag down a motorcycle taxi, jump on the back, and the driver will tell you everything you need to know—they are natural problem solvers. Admittedly, it helps if your problem somehow involves a dearth of hookers, drugs, or field-grade artillery, but these friendly chaps won't rest (nor will they let you off the bike) until you're satisfied.

And that, my friends, is how I found myself outside the Central Market in Phnom Penh, navigating my way around the dangerously overloaded rickshaws, vans, and pickup trucks.

Upon arriving at the market, I was immediately mobbed by truck drivers offering to take me somewhere, anywhere. Many of them tried pulling me and my bike toward their trucks even before I told them where I wanted to go—they would simply nod vigorously and bark, "Yes! Yes!" over and over again. When I finally managed to shout, "Siem Reap!" over the chaos, one of the men jumped jubilantly in the air as if he had just won the coveted Tourist Dollars Lottery. He pulled me toward his already packed truck as his competitors gloomily retreated.

"How much?" I asked the driver.

"Five dollar inside, three outside, two for bike," he told me.

In the back of the truck there were already seventeen or

eighteen people. And when I peeked inside, there were four young women squished into the back, and in the front bucket seat, a mother and her three-year-old child. Where I would sit was not exactly clear.

So I resigned myself to a long, painful ride as I set to the task of securing my bike and the panniers that held all my worldly possessions. I took the saddlebags off my bike and looked around for a place to put them. There was a small roof rack on top of the cab, which seemed to be the only logical choice.

"Okay to put up there? Safe?" I asked the driver.

"No problem, they hold!" he said happily, pointing at two teenage boys climbing up to the roof of the cab.

I was confused. "They're going to hold it where? Where do they sit?"

"Yes, yes, with your bag! No problem!" he sang.

And this was really my first introduction to the madness of Cambodians. They may be insane drivers, but they are surely even more insane as passengers. These guys were actually going to ride on the roof of a moving pickup truck as it sped down the highway.

As I would soon find out, "Riding on Top of Things" seems to be a kind of national sport in Cambodia. Over the next six hours, I saw things that made those two kids look like poster boys for the AMA automobile safety program. There were people driving motorcycles, hauling absurdly large cargo behind them—my personal favourite was a guy carrying a queen-sized mattress on the back of his bike, laid flat like a giant wing as he propelled along at thirty kilometres per hour. On several occasions, I saw Asian Evel Knievels sitting on top of motorbikes, which were, in turn, lashed upright onto the tops of moving buses. But even that paled in comparison to the craziest person I saw—a guy riding on the hood of an overcrowded school bus. Four words, dude: "Take the next bus."

With my bag squared away, I checked back to see where in God's name they were going to put my bike. The obvious answer was where they put everything else. They quickly strapped it to the open gate in the back of the truck. There was already a ton of luggage fixed to it, and when I got back there, they were roping my bike to all the other random stuff. By the time they had finished, it was sticking out at least a metre from the back of the truck. It made me wonder if I would ever see it again.

In a quest for some added insurance, I began chatting with everybody sitting in the back. If I struck up some friendships, maybe they would actually try to prevent it from slipping off the back of the truck if the rope came undone, rather than watch it bounce a few times and get pulverized by the next car. Nobody in the truck spoke English, of course, but they were already staring at me, thanks to the fact that I was a white guy. They evidently thought I was hilarious. I just smiled back, making little cycling motions, pointing at my bike, then clasping my hands together in prayer.

As it turned out, I had nothing to worry about. Somebody tied two baskets of live baby pigs to the outside of my bike, and—just for a little added insurance—I saw three live chickens hanging by their feet from the crossbar. These people had a lot of vested interest in my bike staying on board. Believe me, that bike was going nowhere.

With the luggage secured, I headed back to the cab, pulled open the door, and was again greeted with puzzled stares. It was unclear whether their bemusement stemmed from the fact that I was a white guy taking this particular mode of transport, or whether it was more about me sticking my butt into that cab like the last frat boy in a telephone booth. So I just gave them a wide smile, a loud enthusiastic, "Okay ladies, I'm comin' in!" and a big thumbs up. Not surprisingly, they burst out laughing.

For all my enthusiasm, I still hadn't solved the problem of where I was actually going to sit. The driver swivelled his head around, and then indicated the space between the bucket seats. I was skeptical. "Uhhh ... I'm not even sure that's a seat, friend," I said. But he didn't understand.

I knew I didn't have a whole lot of choice in the matter—the truck was jam packed, and half the livestock in Cambodia was already tied to my bike. So I sucked in my gut and squeezed into a godforsaken space that the good people at Ford never intended as a seat. Basically, I would have no back support for the next six hours. Or leg room. Indeed, I had to straddle the truck's stick shift, which is where things really started to go downhill.

It's true that after travelling in Asia for a while one becomes accustomed to tight and uncomfortable positions. No seat? No problem! No back support? I'll deal with it. No leg room? If you insist. But straddling a stick shift? Whoa, pardner.

Now—picture, if you will, a young man stuck in the cab of a pickup truck in Cambodia with seven other people (plus another nineteen in the back). His left leg is pressed against the woman sitting next to him, his right foot is trying its best not to step on the truck's pedals, and between his legs is a stick shift. And it's one of those ancient stick shifts where you really have to slam it into gear. Bottom line: second and fourth gear? No friends of mine, people … no friends of mine.

Originally, I had figured I would pass the time by playing with the little boy sitting beside me. Instead, what with my unique positioning, I ended up studying the movements of the cars ahead of us like I was doing my PhD on Cambodian Traffic Patterns. I watched intently for starts and stops and, most importantly, for situations when our driver was going to have to slip into second or fourth gear.

After about thirty minutes, the young Cambodian mother and her child fell asleep, the mother with her head on my shoulder, the boy with his head on my thigh. This would have been quite sweet except that it meant I couldn't really move for fear of waking them. So for the next couple of hours, I just prayed for fast, smooth, steady traffic.

I didn't get it.

Like all good things, that trip finally came to an end. It was just under six hours in total, and thankfully the roads between Phnom Penh and Siem Reap have improved dramatically over the years. The drivers untied the chickens and pigs and let me take a couple of photos for the record. At least my bike, if not my manhood, was still intact.

I rode off to the centre of Siem Reap to meet some friends, order an ice-cold banana shake, and pour it down my shorts.

Conor Grennan is an Irish American who spent eight years working in international public policy in Prague and Brussels before taking eighteen months off to travel. His work can also be found in the travel humor anthologies What Color is Your Jockstrap *and* Tales from Nowhere, *and on his web site: www.conorgrennan.com. In his free time, he likes to ride his mountain bike, which still has remnants of chicken shit on it. (Hard to get off, that chicken shit…)*

Whirlybird Applesauce

The dangers of packing fresh fruit on vacation.

By Michael Barnes

I have mixed feelings about helicopters. Sure, they're useful flying contraptions: they can land anywhere; they can hover—it all sounds great. But a ride in a whirlybird turned me against apples. And since apples used to be my favourite fruit, it's been difficult to resolve the troubled relationship I've had with helicopters ever since.

My one and only encounter with these machines was during spring break-up on the Moose River at the southern tip of Ontario's James Bay. For a six-week period in April and May, the river is held hostage by moving pieces of ice. Great chunks of the stuff grind together in the water, cutting off boat traffic from Moose Factory Island to the mainland. At these times, helicopters are the only means of accessing the island.

I was traveling light when I arrived in Moosonee, a small village on the mainland not far from Moose Factory Island. A small suitcase and a six-quart basket of apples were all that accompanied me—hardly the load limit. During freeze-up and break-up, fresh fruit is scarce on the island, so the apples were a contribution to my host's diet.

The machine was one of those small helicopters that vaguely resemble a goldfish bowl with a propeller on top. The pilot waited long enough for me to fasten my seatbelt, then commenced take-off.

I've seen helicopters take off many times. Pilots seem to have two techniques: the straight-up method and the sideways method. I was gambling on the straight-up option, but the pilot fooled me. He flew straight up for about six feet, then veered suddenly to the right and curved aloft. My stomach, however, took the straight-up path, and it wasn't happy until the two routes met again.

The trip itself was just another short ride. Once you have been strapped in a glass bowl and dangled over an ice-filled river, there's really nothing to it. The descent is what made for all the excitement.

The pilot descended onto the landing pad beside the hospital. I guess he had noticed the green hue of my face at takeoff time, so he dropped slowly, setting the bird down gently on its sausage-shaped pontoons.

In that part of the world, payment is cash on the line, so I fished in my wallet for the money to pay the pilot. The nearest place for me to set the basket of apples was on the black control column in the centre of the cockpit.

Helicopters must work on some kind of vibration principle. Everything shakes. While the rotor is spinning, the seats shake, the doors shake, everything shakes. Even the passengers do their own involuntary dance. Maybe that's why they use seat belts—perhaps it's not for protection, but rather to prevent body parts from shaking loose.

Whatever the case, please heed my advice. Don't ever put a basket of apples on a helicopter control column. Have you ever seen those transparent globes that they fill with numbered ping pong balls to mix them up at a bingo game? Well, those apples flew from the basket like a set of bingo balls, only with two small differences. Apples are bigger and harder.

It must have been an entertaining sight for onlookers. An otherwise normal landing was suddenly interrupted by strange behaviour on the part of the pilot and the passenger. Both of them started thrashing around inside the cockpit, weaving, ducking, and periodically clasping their hands to their heads as if they'd just been clobbered by a flying apple or something.

Can you imagine what it feels like to get an apple in the back of the neck just after it has bounced off a windshield? And then, as you go to massage your neck, to be hit square in the jaw with another apple?

Well, speaking from experience, it feels pretty much exactly like you'd imagine.

And so the apples danced, for what seemed an eternity. Eventually the pilot managed to shut down the engine. The apples fell to the ground, clobbering us one last time on their final journey to the floor.

The pilot didn't say much as I scraped what remained of my apples off the interior of his helicopter and paid him. I offered him a few apples and a feeble apology, but he refused my kind gesture, muttering something about danger pay. Naturally, I did not pursue the matter.

Ever since that helicopter ride I've been a little frightened of apples, and I look at the produce section in my local grocery store with a wee bit of trepidation. After all, what if an apple jumps up and clobbers me? It's a terrible thing for a grown man to be afraid of a piece of fruit.

Michael Barnes is the author of fifty books, mostly about the North and police work. He is a member of the Order of Canada, and currently resides in Haliburton, Ontario.

Don't Pick up Hitchhikers

Dad always knows best.

By Christina Cherneskey

I had to get home. Curfew was at ten p.m. and I was close to breaking it. Again. And I really wasn't looking forward to the consequences if I did.

I was fourteen years old and had reached some sort of "cool" status at high school. I was part of the gang that hung out at "the wall"—the place where all the coolest kids could be found—and I had already done some interesting things in my life, like travel to a few faraway places. I knew how to swear and how to make other people laugh. School was okay. I was involved in lots of extracurricular activities. Things were looking good—at least from my end.

But my parents thought I was having too much fun. They hadn't been happy when I had come home the week before smelling a bit like booze. My dad, in particular, seemed to be getting miffed at me more and more frequently.

Despite the incident, I somehow managed to talk my parents into letting me go out on a cold December night, just one week after I had been officially grounded. I was going to see a movie with my friends. Yes, the same friends I had been with when the drinking incident happened. In retrospect, I'm not sure how I convinced them that I was ready for parole.

It was a Thursday night, the only night that stores were open late in Saskatoon. So instead of seeing a movie, we decided to go to the downtown mall. Trust me, it was the coolest thing you could do when the temperature was hovering at minus twenty-five degrees Celsius.

Before we knew it, nine p.m. had come and gone, and so had the 9:15 bus I needed to catch in order to get home on time. And in Saskatoon, when you miss the bus, you miss the boat. Game over.

I considered my options. There weren't many. I had missed the bus, it was close to curfew, and I had lied about where I was going. Not to mention that it was f-f-freezing outside.

We did manage to find a bus that was going partway to my house, but a few minutes later my friends and I found ourselves standing on Eighth Street, one of Saskatoon's main drags, looking helplessly at each other. We were halfway home, and it was only ten minutes to curfew.

I should perhaps mention that I'm the youngest of three girls—three stubborn, single-minded girls. My mother was a child psychologist and my father was a lifelong civic politician and lawyer. He also served on countless committees in Saskatoon, including the Board of Police Commissioners. For Mom and Dad, life was about having a good family who followed the rules. For me, those rules took the fun out of life. Yet I was constantly reminded that one did not break those rules—and if one did, one paid the price.

But let's face it: most fourteen-year-olds are really good at breaking rules. So there I was, stranded on Eighth Street in the middle of winter. I could have called for a ride, but being the youngest I had something to prove, and at that time in my life, proving myself was of great importance. Besides, cell phones didn't exist yet, and finding a pay phone on Eighth Street was not as easy as it might sound.

So I did what any desperate fourteen-year-old girl faced with six months of house arrest would have done. I stuck out my thumb.

For the first time in my life I tried hitchhiking, and soon it was as though I had been doing it for years. I started thinking about how cool I was and about what my friends would tell my other friends at school the next day. I unzipped my jacket a bit, flung back my hair and looked directly into the eyes of the drivers who were whizzing by. I looked back at my friends who were standing on someone's lawn, smoking. I walked backwards a bit, trying to look cool and composed. In my mind, I had already composed a story for my parents about how I had gotten home. I knew I would be a few minutes late, but if I got a ride, I would have a valid excuse.

I was ready for any and all contingencies.

Car after car drove past, and I started to get impatient. I crouched down, trying to make eye contact with the passing drivers, hoping they would see the catchlight of desperation in my eyes. But cars continued to pass without so much as slowing down.

Then I saw a lone car coming down the street. My thumb shot out again as I bent down to eye the driver. I prayed that my frozen red nose and pitiful eyes would be enough to convince him to stop. I made up a little "I'm frozen" dance and clutched my coat to my chest. The situation looked hopeful. As the car came closer, it actually changed lanes as though the driver was going to pull over. I started waving excitedly at my friends while keeping my eyes fixed on the approaching car.

Then I crouched down a bit lower to see who was driving and looked directly into the eyes of … my father. Who looked directly into my eyes. And continued driving.

Then his car stopped. And waited. It sat ominously at the side of the road, exhaust billowing from the tailpipe. I knew that my life was over.

My friends had no idea what had just happened, and they erupted into cheers as they ran toward the car. But before they could reach it, I broke the news. The short-lived celebration became a funeral procession as we trudged toward Dad's car and climbed in.

My father didn't say a word as he drove everyone home. In fact, the deafening silence continued until we walked in the back door of our house. Needless to say, my mother was surprised to see me arriving home with my father, who had just met with the Police Board regarding some policing business. But he didn't say anything to her, and to my knowledge he has never said a word to her about what actually happened or where he picked me up.

He never brought the subject up with me either, and I never brought it up with him. I was so consumed with guilt and fear—not fear of my father so much as fear of what could have happened if we had been picked up by the wrong kind of person—that I could never manage to raise the subject.

One day many years later, the whole incident all but forgotten, I asked Dad if I could borrow the car to go to a movie with some friends. He held out his keys, but as I grabbed for them, he suddenly pulled them back. As I looked into his eyes, a faint grin appeared on his face. "Don't pick up any hitchhikers," he said.

Christina is a broadcast journalist at Newstalk 1010 CFRB Radio *in Toronto. She was raised in Saskatoon, Saskatchewan, where hitchhiking is permitted when the thermometer hits minus 20 Celsius. Christina brings her gift of the gab not only to the CFRB audience, but to* Rogers Television*, where she hosts her own TV show.*

Serendipity

Sometimes the most important people are found in the places we least expect.

By Beverley Abbott

The road has a way of changing you forever. With every highway travelled and every new encounter, your life is enriched permanently, which was certainly the case for me in the summer of 1980.

I was twenty years old and had just finished a year of community college in Ottawa. My dream was to become a social worker and devote my life to helping others, but there was something I needed to do for myself first. Adventure was calling, and I knew that travel would give me an education that could not be provided by any institution.

I had been an easterner all my life, and had only heard about the grandeur of the Rocky Mountains—specifically, Waterton National Park. And so, armed with only a knapsack and a map, I set off on a great Greyhound journey west, much to the chagrin of my loving parents, who were understandably concerned about their only daughter.

Waterton was everything I had envisioned and more. Its endless range of mountains seemed to reach up and touch the sky, and its forever-blowing wind stirred my soul.

After several scary nights spent camping in my flimsy tent, imagining that I was on the menu of every conceivable carnivorous mammal outside, I managed to secure a position at the local employer of choice: the majestic Prince of Wales Hotel. Its ancient dormitories have been home to adventure seekers like myself from all over the globe for decades. My roommate was a similarly aged and like-minded woman from the Maritimes named Twila, and both of us were given the dubious honour of working in the staff cafeteria, affectionately known as "The Slop Shop."

After several weeks, Twila and I started getting itchy feet. Whether it was the wind moving us or too many early mornings of serving slop to our hung-over colleagues, we made the decision to hit the road with our thumbs extended. Although this is something I would never consider today, at the time it seemed like the only reasonable alternative. After all, it was a unique way to experience all that the West had to offer and at the same time be "fiscally responsible." We were certainly not flush with cash from our experience at the Prince of Wales.

Our first destination was Banff, where a friend of Twila's had found work in a local restaurant. After that, our ultimate destination would be the fruit trees of the Okanagan Valley, as we had heard that cherry pickers were in short supply that year.

The first vehicle that stopped was a pickup full of teenagers. They were headed to Calgary for the "Alberta Jam," a large outdoor rock concert featuring a variety of Canadian bands. When they asked if we'd like to join them, the answer was so obvious that Twila and I had no need to consult—we simply responded in stereo with a resounding "Yes!"

After several days of festivities at the Alberta Jam, it was time to hit the highway for Banff. As is so often the case with hitchhiking, the route thus far had been happily circuitous, but now we were on a mission to get a few more dollars into our pockets.

The journey to Banff was straightforward enough. Two rides with vacationing families brought us to the small, bustling town. We arrived hunched over from the weight of our knapsacks, looking more than slightly haggard after days without a shower. Relief, such as it was, came in the form of an offer to work at a Chinese restaurant, with accommodation in a storage closet in the basement. We were really living now!

However, after two weeks of attempting to sleep on a cold concrete floor and counting Campbell's Soup cans rather than sheep, we'd had enough.

We were Okanagan bound!

The many people who picked us up were varied and interesting, each with their own story to tell. But most paled in comparison to one wonderful individual whom we encountered in Peachland, British Columbia. We were sitting outside the Canada Employment Office, feeling disheartened by the news that there was not, in fact, a steady stream of employers looking for the likes of us to assist with harvesting fruit, when we heard a husky voice say, "You gals look like you're lost."

The voice belonged to Ray, a kindly soul and local eccentric who had lived in Peachland for all of his seventy-six years. He was quick to offer us a ride in his '69 pickup to a little piece of land he owned overlooking Lake Okanagan. In exchange for some much-needed help on his farm, he offered us accommodation in his little tent trailer, and regaled us for the next week with stories of his fascinating life and the many people he knew. The generosity Ray offered us has remained with me, and I kept in touch with him regularly until his death in 1998.

As our time with Ray came to a close, Twila and I decided not to push our luck any further. We would make our way back to Waterton, pick up the meagre cheques that awaited us, and head back to our homes and families.

But fate wasn't finished with us yet.

We had just positioned ourselves by the side of the road outside Pincher Creek, Alberta—the last stretch of road before Waterton—when two motorcycles, each with a lone male rider, made their way toward us at significant speed. In jest, we both stuck out our thumbs, and were able to hear one rider yell to the other, "What do you think? Should we pick them up?"

The response was a resounding "No!"—but the first rider was determined, and quickly turned around despite his companion's protest. His friend was forced to do the same, and after reluctantly doubling back on his motorcycle, he pulled up to where we were standing.

"I'm not fat," were the first words out of his mouth. "I just have a lot of clothes on."

This was an odd introduction, I thought, but I must admit that when John took off his helmet my heart fluttered momentarily. He was a very good-looking man.

Twila climbed on with the first fellow, Bob, leaving me to ride with John, the fellow who was apparently *not* fat. The ride began smoothly enough, although it hadn't been easy accommodating all our gear on the motorcycles. I grew more comfortable as the ride progressed, so eventually I decided that I would try to impress John with my knowledge of the area. As he turned around to listen attentively, the visors on our helmets locked together.

Despite our best efforts to separate them, the situation put John's powers of concentration to the test as he tried to focus one eye on the road, while the other focused on me only a few inches away from his face.

Over the twenty-four ensuing years, John has told this tale innumerable times, and he loves to recount that it was at this moment he first stared into my "beautiful brown eyes." He also claims that he knew immediately he'd found the love of his life.

The days, weeks, and months that followed strengthened that initial connection, despite my return to Ottawa and enrolment in university to commence my social work training. After a year apart, I returned to the West by airplane, not thumb, to continue my education and start a life with the man of my dreams.

To this day, I know in my heart that our serendipitous meeting on that roadside, and the frightening entanglement of our helmets, was the work of a force much greater than us. Since that fateful day we have travelled thousands of miles on our motorcycles together, through this wonderful country of ours, and have never again found ourselves in that precarious position. I think we've proved that the road has a will of its own, and that it can weave magic into anyone's life if you are open to its bidding.

Beverley and John live in the Edmonton area with their furred, feathered and finned family. Beverley now has her own set of two wheels, from which she and John continue to explore the highways and byways of western Canada.

Indonesian Freighter

Life is about taking chances.

By Ed Yatscoff

M y Aussie buddy, Damien, and I sat wilting in the shade of a cinder block warehouse wall. A steady stream of brown men, cooking under the sun, carried bales and crates from small freighters along the length of a Jakarta dock. I had figured our sea journey from Jakarta to Singapore would be heaven after enduring third-class rail passage across Java, with the bonus of saving on a bed for three nights.

Tied to the wharf in front of us, however, was a decrepit freighter, a ship ripe for the scrap yard. Damien confirmed that it was our ship. "Stone the bloody crows," he said. "It is ours."

The ship's name painted on the bow was illegible through the streaking rust. We christened it the HMS Scow.

Scattered around us were Europeans, Aussies, one American, and some Brits. They were identified by accents, small flags on their large backpacks, or in the case of the Euros, attitude. A mass of Indonesian men, women, and children with crudely tied bales, bundles, and crates slowly filled the wharf. Many had live chickens trussed to bundles.

When the ship's gangplank lowered, the mass of bodies lurched forward, clambering to get on board, sweeping us along in the mad flow like a river. Somehow all of us westerners ended up at the stern, where backpacks were set down on the blistering steel deck.

"You've got to be bloody joking," griped Damien, upon discovering this spot was both our cabin and bunk. We rolled out our sleeping bags on the cargo hatch and in short order our ship departed, threading across Jakarta's bustling harbour. Two of the crew rigged a large tarp above us. Relief from the heat was immediate.

Damien and I wandered through the freighter wondering where the thousands of Indonesians had disappeared to. We followed a cacophony of voices and noise along passageways deep into the ship. A mass of humanity had crammed into the dim, cavernous hold—an entire village, complete with squawking chickens. Three other holds were no different. Once topside, we counted lifeboats—not enough.

"Perfect for the headlines back home," quipped Damien. "Millions Drown As Overcrowded Ship Capsizes."

"I guess we'll have to sacrifice a chicken to the sea gods," I said.

The few bathrooms were places to avoid as they quickly overflowed into passageways, stinking up the ship. Everything in Southeast Asia was an adventure: getting on the right bus, finding a bed for the night, trying not to offend local customs officers, changing money, finding a post office, and ordering food. Now it was standing in a long line holding our meal vouchers. We were rewarded with a scoop of rice on a banana leaf, topped with two staring fish heads. Everyone ate the rice. The fish heads were either traded with the locals for fruit, or tossed overboard to the ever-present sharks circling in the ship's wake.

I sat along the port rail watching the setting sun turn the Java Sea into liquid copper. A woman sauntered up beside me in a red-flowered sarong, sweeping back her long brown hair. We shared the panorama in awed silence. I'd noticed her early on, along with the tiny red maple leaf on her green backpack. But I was attracted by her sparkling laugh that carried across the deck. She introduced herself as Gloria, her brown eyes smiling invitingly in the fading light.

"Enjoy your dinner?" I asked.

"Well … the rice was good," she replied.

We discussed various ways to eat fish heads without utensils. Suck out the eyes? Chew around the gills?

Gloria was a farm girl from Saskatchewan; the wide open spaces and amber wheat fields were reflected in her easy manner. Like me, she was also travelling with a friend.

I was from southern Ontario, a world apart from hers in the same huge country. After spending over a year travelling, we were both homesick. Canada and home seemed almost an abstract place.

We swapped stories about spending time in Australia as darkness fell like a warm velvet blanket. She had made tea, as a volunteer, for the Queen at the Christchurch Commonwealth

Games. It was a hilarious encounter, she said. I told her I was hell-bound after slamming a car door on an elderly nun's fingers during my first Australian Christmas. We discovered that we may have even been on the same ferry in Sydney.

In the coming days, Gloria and I gravitated toward each other, meeting at the railing and even going so far as to hold hands or casually rub against each other as we walked along. No privacy existed, limiting affections to an occasional stolen kiss—much to the good-natured derision of our friends and fellow backpackers.

At night the flapping of the tarp made for a fitful sleep. I would awaken and gaze across the sleeping forms to where Gloria was lying. Her humour, conversation, and smile had brightened what would have been a smelly and boring trip. In spite of the conditions, I didn't want it to end.

Our ship anchored offshore just north of the equator at Tanjungpinang. Fifty or so Singapore-bound passengers, including us, disembarked onto water taxis while the HMS Scow continued on to Sumatra.

Once ashore, we were directed to a small launch docked in a large lagoon, its surface reflecting the burning equatorial sun. Some of the westerners told us their water taxis had taken them out to sea and demanded money to take them to shore.

While waiting to depart, the fierce heat got to me. I dove into the piss-warm water. After three nights on the stinking freighter it was refreshing. Aboard the launch everyone was pointing at me; some laughed, others were disgusted. Ocean pickles floated in the lagoon. It was a sewage outlet.

Gloria was not impressed.

She stayed inside the cabin with her friend Diane for the half-day Singapore leg. I don't think anybody wanted to be near me. Damien and I sat on the bow, occasionally sprayed by sea foam. We cruised past hundreds of tiny islands that barely rose above sea level, each with a few thatched huts built on stilts. These fishermen lived on a liquid planet, far from shore, their tenuous existence dependent on nature's good graces.

We parted in Singapore. Gloria and her friend were on their way home the long way—via Bangkok, Hong Kong, Japan, and across Russia and Europe by train. Damien and I were blowing in the wind, with England as our distant goal. Travelling overland made us aware of just how big the world really is. The likelihood of meeting up with Gloria again was small. We swapped addresses, promising to keep in touch.

Friendships on the road are quickly struck and can often be intense, but rarely are they revisited.

Farther up the Malaysian Peninsula in Penang, however, we bumped into each other at a small seaside eatery. I invited Gloria and Diane to visit a losmen set back deep in the jungle, where Damien and I were staying. We showed them the captive mongoose that our innkeeper used to get snakes out of the roof rafters, and the giant fruit bats hanging from massive trees like pinecones. After our visit, it never even occurred to us to escort the women back to the road through the dark jungle.

Gloria and Diane were not impressed.

The next day I saw Gloria walking along a beach near Penang with an American fellow I'd also met on the freighter. They were holding hands. Oh yeah, I was jealous! I looked for something in her eyes, in her tone, to reflect our previous connection. There was nothing. So much for mutual affection and chemistry.

I was not impressed.

As luck would have it, we met again in Bangkok. Her hotel had a great pool; mine had bedbugs or some other kind of pestilence. The American was gone. I felt Gloria and I begin to reconnect. Damien and I escorted them around Bangkok to markets and temples. I treated Gloria to a movie and a stroll along the notorious Pat Pong Road in Bangkok's red light district.

She wasn't impressed that I knew the area so well.

My overtures to spend the night with her were quickly quashed. Western girls didn't sleep with western guys in Asia, as men were well known for their promiscuous behaviour.

Damien and I eventually made it to London. I had little money left by that time, and somehow I managed to lose him, quite literally, to a sexy English girl from the Midlands.

After my eighteen-month journey, I returned home to Welland, Ontario, aware of how much I had changed. The town hadn't. My mind had been opened, filled with wonder about all the beauty, poverty, and despair in the world. I had become more self-reliant, more adaptable, and braver. My hometown belonged to the "Flat Earth Society." My job at a rubber plant sank me into a despair of sorts. After a few months, I wrote Gloria on a whim. She wrote back. I was thrilled. It sealed my decision to leave town.

I decided to move to Edmonton for a job. She worked at the CBC in Saskatoon, and on my drive across the Prairies, I worked up the courage to drop in unannounced. She had mentioned something about moving to Calgary, but I had no idea when.

The elevator opened and Gloria stepped out. It felt awkward thrust face to face so quickly. We stood for a moment looking at each other, not really knowing what to say. She wasn't the same woman I had stamped in my memory, the azure Java Sea in the background. She'd swapped her green backpack and sandals for a leather purse and heels. The sarong and T-shirt were now a summer blouse and a tight blue skirt. Her long hair had been trimmed and was somewhat shorter and more stylish. Her deep tropical tan had faded.

But the smile was still there. With a hug, our bodies meshed in familiarity, and the connection returned. Her laugh bridged a million miles of loneliness. Not only that, the timing of our reunion was a gift from the gods. She was moving to Calgary the next morning, where Diane was already established, and we might well have lost touch.

Back at her apartment, I was stunned to see that I was in one of the photos she'd taken of her friend shortly after boarding the ship—before we'd even met. There I sat in the background, writing in my travel journal. It was almost eerie.

The next morning, Gloria tossed her few possessions in my car and we were off toward Alberta. I could only stay with her for a few days. When I dropped her off in downtown Calgary my heart broke.

Nevertheless, we began a "Highway 2 romance," which is what happens in Alberta when one half of a pair lives in Edmonton and the other half lives in Calgary. "Sweet City Woman" played on my car radio as I drove back and forth every weekend, strengthening our connection to the point of love. She made perogies and baked me pies. We took day trips to Banff.

After two months of searching, Gloria still hadn't found work in Calgary. Bad news for her turned out to be great news for me, however, when an Edmonton television station called requesting an interview. They liked what they saw and hired her, and I eagerly helped her move north.

Obviously, something had conspired to bring us together. I decided I had no choice but to ask her to marry me and leave nothing more to chance. If I hadn't, I knew we'd just keep bumping into each other.

Ed Yatscoff has had a number of short stories and travel articles published, and is currently seeking publishers for several novels. He is a captain with Edmonton Fire Rescue and plays drums in a community band. He and Gloria live in Beaumont, Alberta, where he is active in the community.

Public Parking

When a romantic getaway turns into a test of endurance.

By Lesley Monette

Travelling can be a miraculously transformative experience. Can you think of a better way to abandon reality and have your identity hidden secretly within the confines of your suitcase for a few weeks?

A pair of old hiking boots; rain pants and matching jacket; three bras; six pairs of socks; ten pairs of underwear; four T-shirts; two pairs of shorts; one nice evening dress; a bathing suit; and my favourite pair of jeans in the whole world. That's who I was for three weeks in Europe: someone who wanted to see everything that I had never seen before, and in the end, come back transformed. I wanted stories that everyone else seemed to have, stories that would finally fit me perfectly, too.

It was June, and it was hot as we stumbled out of the airport after our flight from Toronto to Barcelona. While the long plane trip had been exhausting, travelling with my husband had definitely helped. He had demanded only the best, and had us sitting in first class both ways.

We were to begin in Spain and then travel through France, England, and Prague before flying back to Canada. I had never travelled so far or been so excited. We had both taken three weeks off work, and had prepared for months in advance. We were ready for anything.

The fact that we ended up in the small town of Sitges was mostly my doing. At the end of our first week in Europe, we decided on having a special evening out to celebrate. Peter, being the stubborn spirit that he sometime is, wanted to eat in one of the highly recommended restaurants of Barcelona. I pointed out that there were many small towns along the coast that would expose us to a more authentic Spanish experience. After a long, drawn-out argument, which I won, we settled on renting a car and driving down the coastline. While my husband, in spite of the sticky Spanish heat, adorned himself in a gorgeous pinstriped suit, I threw on my favourite pair of jeans and a tank top.

Many of the small towns along the coast seemed to dip right into the ocean and disappear. It was a gorgeous sight.

"What about Sitges?" Peter asked, pointing to a large green sign on the side of the road. "It's only thirty kilometres away."

"If it's anything like these other little towns we've been passing, it should be perfect." I fumbled around for my guidebook and flipped it open, but couldn't find Sitges.

"It's not even mentioned in the book," I told him. "I guess we're on our own."

The beauty of Sitges lies in her golden coast. Seventeen beaches line the ocean and glisten with white talcum-powder sand—the kind of sand you dig your feet deep down into and wiggle your toes around until they pop out looking like they're caked in icing sugar. We traced narrow cobblestone roads winding down toward the ocean, and parked the car along the boardwalk.

"This place is incredible," I cooed, skipping over to a fence that separated the city from the ocean. "Take a look at that church!"

Overlooking the main beach was an old stone church. It stood towering over the sea, giving the trendy boardwalk with its palm trees and long beaches an ancient feel. Peter wiped away a bead of sweat and pulled his camera from his pocket, then snapped a picture as I struck a pose against the railing.

We ended up eating at a tiny bistro in the centre of the main piazza, laughing heartily as we tried to read the menus and order dinner using our broken Spanish. Luckily, the restaurant was fairly empty—which, we were told in broken English, was because the Spanish usually eat very late at night.

As we walked back to our rental car, young men and women sat at the sides of the road painting and selling jewellery to passing tourists. Peter, slightly tipsy on the fine Spanish Rioja we had been drinking, rambled on about the exquisite paella and tapas we had eaten. I paid little attention, too busy searching through my purse for the keys.

"… And the best thing is, it's only nine o'clock," he said. "We'll make it back to Barcelona by ten for a drink at the bar. I hear our hotel makes a fantastic dry martini."

He looked over at me with a dazed, happy look on his face, but all I could say was, "The car keys are gone."

*   *   *

The police station in Sitges was small and dirty, with oil-streaked eggshell-white walls. As it was nearly ten o'clock, the station was filled with only a few dozing Spaniards.

Peter woke a small, rotund policeman sleeping in his cubbyhole office. After many failed attempts at communication, one of which involved my husband trying to mimic a steering wheel in a failed game of charades, I intervened.

"Habla Inglés?" I asked, flipping in despair to the "common phrases" section of my guidebook.

"Inglés?" The officer seemed to understand. I nodded as he twitched his thin black moustache, wiped a few crumbs from his stained uniform, and wandered out the door. I stared out into the hallway after him, and Peter fell defeated into a small plastic chair in the corner.

Moments later, the officer returned, followed by a very handsome and tall Spanish man. The man walked straight up to me and planted kisses on both my cheeks.

"Hola!" he said. I blushed a little.

"Do you speak English?" Peter asked, stepping between the two of us.

"Yes, sir, I do. I am the police chief here." He raised a hand toward my husband, who shook it powerfully. "My name is Veno, and this is Fabrizio." He motioned to our *Sancho Panza*, leaning against the doorframe. "How can we be of service?"

I sat next to my husband as he described our predicament. "Obviously," he concluded, "we need to find the car keys so we can drive back to our hotel tonight."

As he finished, I looked up to find Fabrizio lugging a huge gold trunk in through the office door. When the two officers opened it up, our faces fell. The trunk was full to the brim with keys—small silver ones that looked like they were made for lockers, large brass ones that might open a sixteenth-century treasure chest. But nothing that looked like a set of car keys.

Peter jumped out of his seat.

"You expect us to find our keys in … this?" he stammered.

"Unfortunately, these are all the keys that have been collected," said the chief. "If your keys are not here, I don't know how we can be of service."

Peter began to pace back and forth angrily. Ignoring him, I thanked both officers for their help. They nodded their heads, spoke about cheap late-night accommodations, and left us alone in the unbearable heat of the stuffy police station with a huge gold trunk of keys.

Thirty minutes later, with no success, we stumbled out of the police station gasping for fresh air.

"What are we going to do now?" I asked.

Turning around, I came face to face with a gesticulating Fabrizio. He was chattering excitedly in Spanish, gesturing toward a taxi and struggling to compose his words.

"Andreas," he repeated several times. "In piazza. *Puede ayudarle.*"

I pulled out my guidebook and searched for the word *ayudarle*. Fabrizio continued pointing to the taxi, and made the same steering wheel action Peter had used earlier.

"Do you understand what he's saying?" asked Peter.

"Yes, I think so. I think he's saying that someone in the piazza is named Andreas, and that he can help us."

Fabrizio nodded excitedly.

Peter shot Fabrizio a suspicious glance. "That's ridiculous. The only people in the piazza at this hour are tourists and taxi drivers."

But Fabrizio continued to point again at the taxi across the street.

Peter looked exasperated. "Well, we might as well look for this Andreas. I'm not sure what other options we have."

We left Fabrizio behind and began our search. It took us another hour to find the right piazza and the driver Fabrizio had described; we asked about six different men before we finally found Andreas. His face was a mask of wrinkled skin with the consistency of sun-streaked leather, lined with a thin layer of whiskers and silver hair. Something in that face looked calming and familiar.

"Can I help you?" he asked.

"You speak English," I said thankfully.

"I drive taxi, I must speak many languages. People come from all around the world to visit Sitges."

"Of course." I smiled at the old Spaniard as he stepped out of his taxi, hefting an old wooden cane.

"So, where you want to go?"

The three of us approached our small rental car together, and Andreas walked around inspecting its exterior. He opened the hood and took a look at the engine. I pulled at my husband's sleeve and whispered, "How is this going to help find our keys?"

He shrugged.

Andreas turned and began walking back toward his taxi. "Yes, I can start car for you. It is the usual rental, easy to break into."

I ran over to him and asked nervously, "What do you mean, 'easy to break into'?" He popped the trunk to reveal a purple velvet sack containing all sorts of long metal rods and screwdrivers. My palms began to sweat. Peter, on the other hand, seemed quite excited.

"Just relax, honey, this is perfect. We'll jump the car and drive back to the hotel. End of hassle."

I tried to reply but he had turned his attention to Andreas, and the two of them chatted amicably about the art of car thievery.

Andreas picked out a long, black coil of metal and hobbled back toward the rental car, my husband close behind. I followed a few metres further behind, breathing into a paper bag I found by the side of an old hardware store. It was the only thing keeping me from panicking.

Andreas worked the tool into the car door, which unlocked with a small pop!

Peter performed a little dance of joy, and I dropped my bag and hurried over.

"Did he get it?" I asked.

"Oh, so now you're interested, are you?" teased Peter.

Andreas, in the meantime, had positioned himself at the back of the car and was straining to push it under a streetlight. After a few carefully chosen words from me about serving time in a Spanish jail for car theft, my husband reminded me that it was our rental car. His reasoning didn't entirely convince me, but there were few options, so I joined the men at the back of the car to start pushing.

As the three of us inched the car forward, there was a loud click! Peter jumped back in surprise; Andreas stopped and slapped a hand against his forehead, then shuffled off toward his taxi mumbling Spanish profanities under his breath.

I walked around to the front of the car and climbed into the driver's seat. The steering wheel would not budge.

"Well, Einstein," I said, "the steering is now locked."

Andreas returned with a smaller purple satchel full of small files. "I use this metal file like key in the ignition to start car," he said. We looked at him in astonishment and silently nodded.

He went to work with the file in the ignition, shaking the small tool and jamming it deeper and deeper into the opening. Peter watched in amazement, while I wandered away from the scene.

Hearing the sound of a door opening behind me, I turned to see a small white-haired man walk out of the hardware store, then run toward me holding out a small set of silver keys. My face lit up as I recognized them.

"Peter, look! It's our keys!" I cried out so loudly that it surprised Andreas, who jerked his hand away from the ignition. The metal file broke in two with a snap! One small portion of it was now jammed in the ignition, the other piece in Andreas's hand.

"Oh my God," I moaned. I leaned back against the hardware store window, feeling completely worn out.

The next thing I knew, the little shopkeeper was pulling a large vacuum cleaner out of his store. Andreas shrugged his shoulders and watched the man thread a long extension cord from his shop to the vacuum, then begin taping the hose to the car's ignition. I walked over to my husband, who was sitting on the ground beside a dim streetlight. He put his hand on my shoulder, and as I plopped down next to him, the vacuum roared to life.

After several minutes of trying in vain to suck the file from the ignition with the shopkeeper's vacuum, the two men began arguing about what to do next. Hands flailed and words flew. With a swift dismissal, the man from the hardware store ran back inside, returning a few seconds later with a large magnet that the two men now attempted to use to pull the piece of metal out of the ignition.

The sight was so overwhelming that we broke out laughing until tears streamed down our faces. We were both exhausted.

Finally, realizing how ridiculous the situation had become, Peter stood up to put an end to the performance. After thanking Andreas and the storeowner for their help, we quickly discovered that the only fitting way to extend our gratitude was by sending them off with a hand full of pesetas. As the two men disappeared into the night, Peter and I walked to our poor little rental car, pushed the seats down as far as they would go, and settled in for a long and fitful sleep.

In the morning we located a rental car company within walking distance and returned to our car with one of their employees. Vincente inspected the car, pointing out the bend in the door frame and the metal file jammed into the ignition. Peter stood behind him nervously; we had yet to recount the story of our night in Sitges.

"We need to get back to Barcelona quickly," Peter told Vincente, "but the keys no longer work, as you can see." He motioned to the ignition, while I paced back and forth in the background.

"The door was open, so we slept in the car last night," he added, trying to hide his anxiety about damage charges.

Vincente finished his inspection and shook his head in astonishment.

"Somebody has tried to steal this car," he said.

"No!" we replied, feigning innocence.

"Not to worry," Vincente reassured us. "I will get you a new one."

I glanced at Peter with a feeble smile, feeling slightly guilty. "That would be fantastic," I said. "Thank you so much."

Peter winked at me, and the three of us returned to the rental hut to sign the papers and leave our story—and the town of Sitges—behind.

Weeks later, I received my pictures from the developer and eagerly went through them. Red double-decker buses in England; the Eiffel Tower in France; the castles and rivers of Prague. They were so beautiful, and all of them, Peter and I had shared together.

One picture, however, really caught my eye. It was a simple shot that my husband had taken of me. I was standing against the railing, overlooking the ocean at Sitges. No treasure chest full of keys. No vacuum-wielding shopkeepers. Just me. Alone by the beach. Wearing my favourite pair of jeans in the whole world.

Since the Sitges incident, Lesley has been working as manager of IT at Branksome Hall Secondary School in Toronto. She still loves to travel, and has been spotted with her partner Tito in New Zealand, Brazil and Portugal. While her most recent adventures involve fighting forest fires in the Algarve, Lesley says she will never give up the comforts of her cozy home in Toronto

Molly and Me

A man's best friend is not easily replaced.

By Mark Fisher

It was during a road trip to Alberta, before my last year of high school, that I met Jedi, a Siberian husky who belonged to my friend Peter. I had wanted a dog all my life, but was never allowed to have one because my younger sisters had asthma. I was so taken with Jedi that I wanted to stay in Alberta for my last year of high school, but unfortunately, Ontario and Alberta have very different education systems. Just before school started, I realized that I had to move back home.

I was mostly unhappy for the next four months. Indeed, Christmas Day was probably the unhappiest day of my life … until eight o'clock that evening, when my father sent me outside to get something from the van. Nestled between the two front seats on a pillow was a puppy. She was black and white, and was the tiniest and softest puppy I had ever seen or touched.

It didn't take us long to bond, and from that day forward Molly and I were inseparable. We went everywhere together—grocery stores, the mall, parks, even for short road trips. She was just like me in that she loved to be in the car, loved to be moving, loved new faces and places. So when I decided to take a road trip to the

Maritimes with my friend Greg, there wasn't any question as to whether or not Molly was coming.

It was a chilly January morning when Greg and I loaded up my old '88 Plymouth Voyager, "the Wham." We had given it this nickname for the strange rumbling noises it sometimes made, its finicky personality, and the fact that its heater didn't work. We stopped in Ottawa and Montreal to visit friends, but it got so cold in Montreal that we were stranded there for almost two days before the Wham would start again.

We detoured through Halifax to visit my sister and her boyfriend before pressing on to Prince Edward Island. There is a beautiful bed and breakfast in Crapaud, PEI owned by the Wells family, old friends of my dad's. With true Maritime hospitality, they invited us in, offered us a room and a meal, and even found a place for Molly to sleep. They had two dogs of their own, Maple and Jester, and those dogs treated Molly like a long-lost friend. The three of them played outside in the snow for hours.

The next day, we took the Wham for a tour of the island. We wanted to see the ocean, even though it was mostly frozen at that time of year. We eventually found a side road that looked promising, so we turned and followed it for a short distance, only to get stuck in a snowdrift about halfway down the road. So Greg and I climbed out of the van and started using whatever we could find to remove the snow from underneath and around the wheels. The most useful utensils were a window scraper and a boot, which didn't give us a lot to work with.

After about an hour of digging, our industriousness began to flag. We gave up and decided to call the Canadian Automobile Association on my cell phone. They replied that it would be an hour before they could get there, so we decided to walk down to the ocean—after all, that was why we were there in the first place. It was only about five hundred metres to the edge of the ocean, and when we arrived, we looked expectantly over the edge of a small cliff. Directly below us was a small rabbit.

Now, a rabbit didn't appeal much to Greg or me, but to Molly the rabbit looked like a new friend (or perhaps dinner). Before I could restrain her, she shot over the edge of that cliff like a black rocket and bounded out across the frozen ocean after the fleeing rabbit. We tried calling her back numerous times, but she was already too far away. And it was then that CAA decided to show up.

The tow truck driver hooked up chains and pulled the Wham out of the snowdrift, but as soon as he had removed the chains, he wanted to get paid. I didn't have enough cash on me so I needed to pay with a credit card; when I told the driver, he informed me that we would have to go back to his shop to pay. I told him that I wasn't ready because I was waiting for my dog to come back, but he didn't care. So we followed him to his shop, about ten minutes down the road, paid him as quickly as possible, and then returned to the same spot to try to find Molly.

By this time, she was nowhere in sight.

We searched for more than two hours until it got dark. Worse yet, we had to leave that night because earlier that day I had received a phone call from my mom, who told me that my grandfather was very ill. She had asked me to return home, and I had promised we would leave that evening. On top of that, a terrible storm was blowing in off the coast. It was in these conditions that Greg and I started the long and lonely trek home.

The next morning, after driving all night, we finally stopped to eat and to call the Wells family back in Crapaud. When we told them Molly was missing, Mr. Wells offered to do everything he could to help find her. He called the local CBC radio station and asked them to send out a message; he also called all the people who lived in the area to let them know that Molly was missing and that she wasn't a coyote. He was worried that somebody might shoot first and ask questions later. My sister Nicole pitched in from her apartment in Halifax, posting a message on the SPCA web site.

When Greg and I limped into Ottawa two days later, Molly was still missing and Prince Edward Island was being hit with a terrible storm. I have to admit that I didn't hold out much hope.

Then my cell phone rang. It was Mr. Wells. He had just received a call from some people who lived about a forty-five-minute drive from his bed and breakfast. They had heard the radio broadcast and had recognized Molly when she came wandering through their yard. They had lured her into their garage and were feeding her a nice warm meal. Best of all, she was perfectly healthy—just a little jittery and scared.

Not five minutes after that call, my Mom phoned to tell me that my grandfather was going to be okay.

Needless to say, I turned to Greg and said, "Well, let's go back to Crapaud."

"Are you freakin' nuts?" was his response.

He wasn't coming. I can't say I blame him. Driving fifteen hours east for the second time in a week in a vehicle with no heat … I suppose that classifies as slightly crazy.

Fortunately, another friend of mine who happened to be living in Ottawa wanted to come. So we left at about nine that night and showed up at Mr. Wells's house at around six the next evening. Knocking on his door was one of the greatest feelings I've ever had.

Molly seemed to know that it was me at the door, because she came bounding out into the front room before the door was even open. As soon as it did open, she leapt up with her front paws on my shoulders and started yelping loudly. There aren't many better feelings in life than that.

We stayed at the Wells's for dinner that evening, along with Jim and Shirley, the couple who had rescued Molly. They had heard about the Wells's bed and breakfast, but had never been there. They explained that Molly had gotten so hungry that she was trying to eat some garbage near their house, so they had put some cat food on a blanket in the garage, hoping to tempt her inside. Luckily, it worked, and eventually they got her to eat out of their hands. They told me she was a wonderful dog.

After thanking Jim and Shirley a million times, we finally left Prince Edward Island on our final journey back to Ontario.

It turned out to be the greatest trip I've ever taken, and since then I've never gone anywhere without telling Molly how much I love her.

Mark Fisher recently moved to Olds, Alberta where works as a pipeliner. Molly is temporarily living in Ontario with Mark's parents until he can find a proper home for both of them. They still love travelling together.

Family Ties

When a detour brings you unexpectedly home.

By Michael L. Plouffe

The summer of 1978 is one that I will never forget. In June of that year I turned seventeen, and with one year of high school left, I decided to hitchhike west for the summer—solo.

I knew that the road can get pretty lonely when you're stuck by yourself on some desolate highway in the middle of nowhere, but I was looking forward to the challenge and adventure. I had always dreamed of seeing the Rocky Mountains, and this would be my summer to do it.

Shortly after school ended, I left southern Ontario with my thumb in the air. The weather was sunny and clear and the long-range forecast was even better. After four days of hitchhiking and some great rides, I found myself about ten miles east of Thunder Bay. That's when a pleasant fellow named Gary Deschamp stopped to offer me a lift. He said that he could take me into town, where it would be easier for me to catch a ride, but first he had to make a quick stop at home to pick up his wallet, which he had forgotten.

Gary lived on a farm with his parents, his sister Yvonne, and his two brothers—Claude and Danny. When we arrived at their home, he invited me in to meet everyone. His mother Irene smiled brilliantly from beneath a mane of beautiful red hair and asked if I would stay for supper. There was plenty to eat, she told me, and having a new face in the house would be a welcome change.

I accepted gratefully, looking forward to a good home-cooked meal—something I hadn't had in a while. The peanut butter and jam sandwiches and canned food I had been eating for the last few days were starting to lose their appeal

That evening, we feasted on a delicious pot roast dinner, sharing stories and laughing around the supper table. It wasn't long before the family suggested I stay for the night. Gary told me that he could drive me to the highway first thing in the morning. I was more than happy to stay, as I was staggering under the weight of a full stomach and was starting to feel a bit sleepy.

I got to know those folks quite well that evening, and they got to know me. Mrs. Deschamp nicknamed me "Frenchie" because of my French Canadian background and because I was bilingual. She was a very kind lady who possessed a gentleness that I've seen in very few people. In fact, everyone in that family had a special quality about them.

The invitation kept getting better and better. Just before bed that evening, the family invited me to stay and work on the farm for a few days to earn some money to support my travels. Mr. Deschamp said that I could use either the pickup truck or his brand new '78 Trans Am to run errands for the family. I felt pleased and fortunate that he trusted me so much.

Again I accepted their offer, but informed them that I wasn't sure how long I would stay. I told them that I didn't want to commit to something like this when I knew, as they did, that thumbing my way to the mountains was what I really wanted to do.

Over the next couple of weeks I worked side by side with the Deschamp children. There was always plenty to do, as I expect is the case with most farms during the summer months. A few times, I noticed that Mrs. Deschamp looked quite tired. I asked her about it, but she chalked it up to the busyness of the season.

One morning Yvonne and I went into town to get some groceries while the family worked outdoors. When we arrived back at the house, we went inside to unpack. Yvonne called out to her mom but there was no answer. She called out a second time, but there was still no answer.

Mrs. Deschamp was usually in the house, so we were surprised not to hear from her. "Maybe she's out in the garden," said Yvonne.

A few minutes later, Yvonne found her mother lying in bed. Mrs. Deschamp appeared to be sleeping, but when Yvonne tried to wake her up, she didn't respond. Yvonne yelled for me to call an ambulance, which I did immediately.

It took the drivers about fifteen minutes to arrive, because of the farm's location in the country. The attendants performed CPR on Mrs. Deschamp, and then lifted her onto a stretcher and placed her in the back of the ambulance. The family and I followed close behind.

Two weeks after I arrived in Thunder Bay and met this kind family, Mrs. Irene Deschamp passed away. She had slipped into a coma at the house, and died the next day at the hospital. The cause of death was cancer.

It must have taken one very strong woman to keep going the way she had. She rarely took a break and never complained of pain. She had always put her family ahead of her own well-being.

The family asked me to be a pallbearer at her funeral, which was a great honour for me. It meant a lot to them, so I'm sure it would have meant a lot to Mrs. Deschamp. We all felt she was watching over us.

I worked for another month on their farm, but knew that I soon had to leave. Summer holidays were over and I had to return to southern Ontario to finish my last year of high school. I would have to put off my trip to the Rocky Mountains for at least another year, but that was fine with me.

The night before I left, we had an emotional farewell party. The family told me that Mrs. Deschamp thought of me as one of her own children, as a member of her family. They thanked me profusely for the help that I had given them. I thanked them for the pleasure of getting to know such a wonderful family. I knew that this summer would become one of the greatest memories of my life.

Mr. Deschamp offered to buy me a train ticket for my safe return home, but I declined. I wanted to finish the trip using my thumb, the same way that I had started. Although I knew it would be a long trek back—especially with all the memories of that summer—I still wanted to hitchhike. The road is a perfect place for introspection and healing, and it was there that I would begin to reconcile the memories of five new friends with the sudden and tragic loss of another.

Michael Plouffe is a writer from Kitchener, Ontario, where he lives with his wife and two daughters.

Cheating the Grim Reaper

How many lives does a man have?

By Matt Jackson

George Hunter has defied death so many times over the past fifty years, his stories verge on the miraculous.

Imagine going for a sightseeing flight in a small, fixed-wing airplane. The pilot is flying over Edmonton's North Saskatchewan River Valley, and you are sitting comfortably in your seat. You're a professional photographer, so the passenger's-side door has been removed for easy shooting. The camera is in front of your eyes, your finger is merrily clicking the shutter button, and the breathtaking cityscape is passing under a magnificent arc of blue sky. You are completely absorbed.

Then the pilot swerves to avoid hitting a bird.

Suddenly, the wind has really picked up. When you glance away from your camera, you realize that you are now outside the airplane. Somehow your camera strap has wrenched your seatbelt free and, thanks to the pilot's fancy aerobatics, you have been thrown out. You are now balanced precariously on one of the wing struts, and your legs are dangling over several hundred metres of empty air.

Looking over your shoulder, you see the pilot. His face is sheet white and he is frantically motioning at you NOT TO MOVE! Like, hell! If you're anything like George Hunter, you have other priorities. First, pass your camera to the pilot so your equipment is safe. Second, climb back inside the airplane at any cost!

Unfortunately, with the wind howling so loudly, Hunter and the pilot couldn't hear each other. The pilot wanted to land the airplane, but with hand gestures, Hunter made it clear that he wanted inside. So the pilot banked the plane on its side, thereby recruiting gravity to help save Hunter's skin. He banked it once, twice, three times, but each time a gust of wind nearly ripped Hunter from his perch. Four times the pilot banked the plane, then five. Eventually, miraculously, Hunter climbed back into the cockpit. They landed safely and took a much-deserved break for lunch.

Forty years later, Hunter still has nightmares about that flight.

That wasn't the first or the last time George Hunter would cheat the Grim Reaper. As a photojournalist, he travels the world to capture images of the people, places, and things that make our planet so diverse and interesting. He has crossed Canada at least a hundred times and visited more than a hundred and twenty countries since the early 1940s. Quite by accident, this has sometimes put him in harm's way.

There was the time, while travelling through Afghanistan in a Land Rover, that his driver missed a curve and careened down a steep, boulder-strewn embankment at full speed. In Iran, he was chased by a whip-wielding cameleer after attempting to photograph a caravan of veiled woman. And on another trip to Afghanistan, he made it to the Kabul airport on the day the Russians invaded, minutes before the last flight took off.

Hunter has also had a few close encounters with boats and other airplanes. He once dead-stick landed his Cessna 180 after the engine quit in mid-flight. On another occasion, a chartered Navajo he was on ran out of fuel, and the pilot barely made the runway at Pearson International Airport. In Montreal, after photographing Expo '67 from a helicopter, the pilot landed to drop him off; an hour later it malfunctioned and crashed, killing both the pilot and engineer. On yet another occasion, he spent a summer in the High Arctic aboard the Hudson's Bay Company supply ship Nascopie. The ship dropped Hunter in Montreal, and sank on its next voyage.

While those were all dangerous situations, the closest call Hunter ever had was probably while photographing a topless tribeswoman in Liberia for a magazine assignment. He was later told by his host that if he had so much as touched the girl's shoulder—as photographers often do when directing a subject—he would have been hauled off to the jungle by her father's tribesmen to become the girl's husband.

And if that had happened, George's partner Patricia might well have tracked him down and killed him!

George Hunter was one of the first photographers inducted into the Royal Canadian Academy of Arts, and in 2001 he was presented with a lifetime achievement award from the Canadian Association of Photographers and Illustrators. More recently, Hunter has produced an exhibition of his photographs that has been featured at several galleries, including the Las Vegas Art Museum in the summer of 2005.

Follow the Red Breaks Road

A really bad day in southern Utah.

By Stephen Legault

"Do you think we can get down that?"

I was sitting behind the wheel of "Toro Azul," my trusted and dependable 1989 Toyota SR5, gripping the wheel with white knuckles. The road sloped down at a 15-percent grade, even though the road itself was anything but graded. It was sandy and deeply rutted, and in addition to the downward pitch, the whole road listed to one side, tilting precariously toward an arroyo. An arroyo is a dry wash that once or maybe twice a year floods with water the colour of blood, and then goes dry.

"Do you think we can get down that?"

Greer Chesher was sitting silently beside me, her border collie Bo at her feet. It was early spring, and we were exploring the Escalante-Grand Staircase National Monument, a 1.9-million-acre swath of wilderness in south-central Utah. Greer was doing research for a book on the Monument and I was along for the ride, such as it was. Greer and I met in the early 1990s when she worked as a ranger at Grand Canyon National Park and I was a volunteer there. We'd stayed in touch, and when I wanted to spend a month in the Escalante, she agreed to show me around.

And now we were driving down the Red Breaks Road, which is really just a couple of sandy ruts that snake across the desert— down around stunted juniper trees, and up over bare red rocks. We were trying to get as close as possible to a place called the V, which is where Harris Wash meets the Escalante River. When we reached a point where we could drive no further, we planned to hike the remaining distance.

It should have occurred to me that *this* was that point. But it didn't. "Do you think we can get down that?" I repeated again.

Slowly but cheerfully Greer said, "Yeah, we can get down that."

What I didn't think about, at least until we were down, was—gravity being what it is—could we get back *up* that?

I shifted into first and crept down the grade in four-wheel drive, leaning to the right to avoid being pressed against the driver's side door, steering to keep the tires in the ruts of the road. The moment we were down, I knew that getting back up was going to be a serious problem. I should have just cut to the chase, turned around, and begun the twelve-hour ordeal of driving those twenty metres of road right then and there. Instead we drove on for another two kilometres, parked where the ruts disappeared into slick rock cliffs, and wandered over the canyon country toward the V. We didn't make it, for whatever reason. That isn't important now. Instead, we rendezvoused with the truck an hour later and began the return journey.

When we got to the place where the road was perched on the edge of the dry wash, I stopped. That was a mistake. If I was an experienced off-highway driver I would have just kept driving, and might possibly have used momentum, horsepower, and a devil-may-care attitude to make it to the top of the grade. But I didn't. The image of the sand giving out under the truck, and Greer, Bo, and I tumbling sideways into the wash made me let up on the gas and roll to a stop. The fall wouldn't have killed us. But we were sixty-five kilometres from the town of Escalante—population four hundred, including dogs—and I was rather attached to my truck. I didn't want this arroyo to become henceforth known as Legault Wash with my battered truck as a monument to my stupidity. Besides, the thought of hiking to Escalante and calling my insurance broker with the news was too much.

I geared down into compound low and began to creep up the grade, hardly touching the gas. Even at this snail's pace the tires dug into the loose blow sand, and we ground to a halt. I backed down—nerves failing at the pitch and angle of the road—and tried again, this time giving the truck a little more gas. We went up. We stopped. We tried again. Once again the truck's tires dug into the sand.

I was cursing.

Back down. This time we got out to survey the scene. The sand was loose and dry, and was blowing in from all around.

We tried a few more times, with me nervously eyeing the dry wash six metres below. It seemed to loom out of the passenger's window.

What came next was an hour or two of roadwork. We hauled rocks from the wash and the surrounding desert, and then found loose brush to build up the road to give the truck some purchase. The wind picked up and blew in more sand, burning our eyes and filling our hair with grit. It was exhausting work. And all the while there was the nagging concern that we might be stuck at the end of a road that sees maybe one or two vehicles a week (or less, who knows!).

When we had enough debris that we thought it could support our weight, we mounted up and took a bit of a run at it. We climbed nearly to the top, the truck swaying back and forth, the engine revving as it worked hard to keep its momentum. Just as we reached the top, however, our handiwork gave out. The tires left the rutted tracks and dug deeply into the sand. We lurched to a halt yet again. I tried to reverse, but couldn't. I switched to compound low. Nothing. We were stuck deep this time.

As soon as I stepped out of the truck I could see that we were going nowhere. On the driver's side, the back wheels were pushed to the very top of their wells and were half buried in sand. On the passenger's side, there was a metre gap between the top of the wheel and the bottom of the well, and it was likewise buried. The axle was completely underground.

I was hiking.

Greer and Bo guarded the truck as I began the walk toward Greer's vehicle—also a Toyota SR5 (our expedition was not sponsored)—parked about ten kilometres away. The plan was to return with her truck and use it to pull mine from the sandy quagmire.

At the trailhead for Harris Wash I flagged down some hikers and they offered to drive me to Greer's truck a few kilometres away. One of them had been stung by a scorpion and they were on their way into Escalante to find medical attention. It looked like the patient would live, but I offered my snake-bite kit in a friendly gesture.

I started back with Greer's truck, over the rocky and pitted road as far as Harris Wash, then down through the creek and up past the sign that warned travellers on the Red Breaks Road that they must have four-wheel drive.

Somebody once told me that four-wheel drive just gets you stuck deeper, further from home. I was beginning to see their point.

As I drove Greer's truck back toward my own, I noticed with some dismay that the tracks from our morning's drive were already gone, blown over as more sand drifted across the pathway. I sighed heavily.

Once again, down and around stunted juniper trees and up over the slick rock, I finally got to the place where my truck rested axle deep in the sand. We hooked up a sturdy towrope, and I got into my truck while Greer heaved with hers. Nothing. We were in too deep, and her four-cylinder SR5 lacked the chutzpah to pluck mine from the desert's greedy clutches.

We were driving.

We made our way in Greer's truck over the sixty-five kilometres of sand, rock, ruts, and finally asphalt, to Escalante. We ate a pizza and drank coffee at the town's first espresso bar—a sign of the times, with the creation of the Monument attracting new business to this tiny town. And then we called *the* tow truck. There was only one.

Greer suggested offering one of the sturdy Escalante men—with a muscular Ford, Chevy, or Dodge truck—a hundred bucks to drive out into the desert and pull my dinky import from the clutches of the Monument, but I lacked the guts to ask anybody. I always felt out of place in Escalante with a truck that was so small and so quiet.

That's when Darrell showed up.

My first response was one of tremendous relief. The tow truck was massive. Its wheels—all six of them—were up to my shoulders! Good news, I thought. This rig will surely do the trick.

When Darrell emerged from the cab to discuss the particulars of our situation, I noted that he looked ready enough, too. He smiled a wide grin and I saw he was missing two teeth on the top and two on the bottom, just about where you might land a well-placed punch. Excellent. He either fought enough not to care, or so rarely that he was really bad at it.

I drove with Greer while Darrell followed behind. We had to stop at the Conoco on the way out of town so Darrell could pick up a friend who could help with the job. That's when I met Steve. He was another affable chap, and most of his teeth were present and accounted for.

On the way, we dropped Greer and her truck at the trailer we had dubbed the "Adventure Pod." I climbed in with Steve and Darrell. We were leaving Greer behind, because there was no sense in getting two Toyotas stuck. It's not like there was a two-for-one towing deal in Escalante that day.

We groaned along in low gear, bouncing over the rocks and ruts of the road to Harris Wash. I inquired after the workings of the big rig, and learned that indeed it was four-wheel drive, but all the wheels that drove were in the back. The two front wheels were for steering only. Then and there I should have seen the trouble brewing.

As we crossed the wash they offered me a cold beer from the back of the truck, which I accepted and ruminated over. Darrell couldn't drink, a condition of his recent parole from prison.

On we drove, further into the desert. Up over the slick rock we ranged, down and around those stunted junipers and through the blowing sand. By this time it was late afternoon and the wind was really starting to howl. Sundown was just a few hours away. Ahead of us was the last stretch of sandy road before the steep decline, the wash, and my truck. We drove headlong into it … and stopped. The front wheels of the massive rig burrowed into the soft sand while the back wheels spun and we were rendered motionless.

Now the tow truck was stuck.

We clambered out and found some rocks and brush, and then used a couple of four-by-fours that Darrell had on the back of his truck for just this sort of situation. We tried again and made a solid two metres before the rig burrowed into the sand again, hub deep in the powdery grit.

Suddenly the couple of hundred metres between us and my Toyota seemed like the distance from Earth to the moon. For two hours we dug, hauled rocks, moved the four-by-fours, gunned the engine, lurched forward, dug in again, and repeated. Each round we made a metre of progress. Once we even drove five metres with loud, raucous cheering before sinking back into the desert. In short, we bonded. Eventually we had to tie bandanas over our faces to keep the blowing sand from accumulating in our noses and mouths. Then we hauled more rocks, reorganizing the desert as we went.

When we finally reached my Toyota it took all of a minute to pluck it from the Monument's greedy fist. It popped out like a cork. I pulled the top from a couple of Mormon 3.5-per cent microbrews, and those of us not on parole enjoyed them, the watery suds washing bits of sand and grit down our gullets.

But we didn't care. We three stood side by side looking back over the road we had just spent several hours transforming. It looked as if it had been carpet bombed. The sandy ruts were churned up a metre deep from the tow truck's massive tires.

"I can't drive my truck over that road," I finally said.

"Man, just drive it like they do in the commercials," replied Darrell.

I didn't have the heart to tell these fellows I had never actually seen a Toyota commercial. So I handed the keys to Steve.

I've never seen my truck do the things Steve made it do that evening. Somehow he got it going fast enough to surf over much of the loose sand, and once when he did get stuck, he shifted into compound low so fast that the momentum of the truck seemed to propel it out of trouble again.

For his part, Darrell pointed the tow truck toward the side of the road and roared across the desert, avoiding the hazard altogether. I groaned at the thought of the hardworking men and women at the Southern Utah Wilderness Alliance ever learning of my malfeasance.

Then I remembered I was standing alone in the desert. Steve was sitting behind the wheel of my truck and Darrell behind the wheel of the tow truck. We were sixty-five kilometres from town and the banjos were silent. I hurried to catch up, congratulated Steve on an impressive display of manly driving, and resumed control of Toro Azul.

In the failing light and blowing sand we made our way back toward Harris Wash. But our misadventure was not yet complete. Remember the down and around the stunted juniper part? Well, the down and around went fine on the way back, with me in the lead and the boys following close behind. But as I gunned the Toyota on the uphill side (I was emboldened by Steve's driving and the thought of what a Toyota commercial must look like) all the gear in the back of my truck slammed against the tailgate. The next thing I knew it had popped open, spilling its contents in the middle of the road.

I pleaded in my mind for Darrell to just run over it, but he didn't. He stopped. And didn't get started again.

I was weeping.

More brush, more rocks, more deep and abiding guilt. It took us another hour to free the tow truck from the incline that had marooned it. The winch came in handy. It's amazing how sturdy a stunted juniper tree is.

It was past ten o'clock when we finally reached Greer's Adventure Pod. She handed me what money she had and I drove ahead of my new friends to Escalante, singing the saddest Ian Tyson songs I could think of as the wind buffeted my Blue Bull.

At the town's only bank machine I took out all the cash I could—Darrell could take neither cheque nor credit card—and paid nearly $500 US for the privilege of their assistance that afternoon. I gave them each a $20 tip—all the cash I had left. Then we parted.

I stopped at the Conoco for more beer, courtesy of Visa, and finally reached the Adventure Pod. It was almost midnight. With a great deal of satisfaction I slid into my sleeping bag, but as I closed my eyes I could feel the sand grating over my corneas. The following morning we drove back into town to shower and I deposited bright red sand from the Escalante Monument into the corners of my shower stall.

Two days later we were driving out to Egypt Point, over a washboard road, when my muffler, loosened after being buried in the sand and unceremoniously wrenched from the desert, fell off. Then I drove over it.

At least I can now take some comfort in the fact that, braying like a jackass, my truck fits in perfectly around Escalante.

Stephen Legault is a writer, photographer, and environmental activist who lives in Victoria, British Columbia. His first book, Carry Tiger to Mountain: the Tao te Ching for Activists *was published by Arsenal Pulp Press in June 2006. Greer Chesher's book—*Heart of the Desert Wild—*was published in 2000. Stephen's Toyota SR5 blew a head gasket climbing a steep mountain pass and was sold for scrap in late 2004. To appease his guilt, he is donating the fee for this story to the Southern Utah Wilderness Association.*

Motorcycle Therapy

Riding a chrome steed through Central America is
not for the faint of heart.

By Jeremy Kroeker

B efore leaving Canada, I carefully studied the travel advisories
for every country between Mexico and Panama. They all said
basically the same thing (and I'm paraphrasing here): "Stay home.
If you are stupid enough to travel in Central America, you will be
kidnapped, sodomized, and killed, but not necessarily in that order.
Certainly don't drive (you idiot), but if you must drive, keep your
windows rolled up and doors locked at all times."

That last bit of advice caught my attention, perhaps because
my friend Trevor and I were planning to ride from Calgary to
Panama City via motorcycle, without benefit of windows or doors.
After much debate, and despite the grim predictions, we decided
to go anyway.

One of the first things we learned after crossing the Mexican
border is that travel advisories tend to overshoot the mark in cases
where safety is concerned. They do, however, fall a bit short in
the category of useful specifics. Consider the following a sort
of anecdotal motorcycle supplement to Central American travel
advisories. When you drive through the region on a motorcycle,

there truly is a plethora of ways you can potentially maim or kill yourself.

I'll never forget our first day in El Salvador. A warm wind snapped at my nylon jacket while we were riding along the country's majestic coastal highway. It was a perfect moment. I could see Trevor riding in front of me, silhouetted against the glistening Pacific Ocean when, suddenly, something large eclipsed the sun. Slowly, deliberately, I turned my gaze to check my rear view mirror and gasped at what I saw.

The black circular frame of my mirror contained nothing but one enormous headlight of a transport truck; it was riding my tail and closing the distance fast. The guy was so close I could almost touch his bumper, and for reasons I can't explain, I decided to try.

Somehow I managed to twist myself around, keeping my right hand steady on the throttle to maintain a delicate equilibrium. Resting my torso on the backpack strapped to my rear seat and reaching as far back as I could with my left arm, I extended my index finger. I could not touch the bumper, so—and this I really can't explain—I gently *rolled back the throttle*. The look of horror and bewilderment on the driver's face as he slammed on his brakes was very entertaining and, instantly, I had plenty of room. That's what I call fighting fire with fire; in order to negotiate with crazy drivers you have to be a little crazy yourself.

Oddly enough, the same principle applies to navigation in the face of inadequate signage, especially in Mexico. On one occasion we had been carefully following signs for Tecoman until the signs suddenly vanished on the outskirts of Manzanillo. It was as if the

Department of Highways went, "Well, we've done all we can do. If they can't find Tecoman on their own from here, they never had a chance."

Imagine if this happened in Canada. You're a foreigner travelling from Calgary to Toronto and the last sign as you approach Winnipeg reads: "Toronto 2,400 kilometres." You pass several key, unmarked intersections. The sun goes down. You admit that you are lost. Now if you're lucky, you wind up in the Exchange district, where friendly Manitobans will direct you to a local pub. If you are unlucky, you wind up in the Murder 500 Block where members of the Manitoba Warriors will instruct you on how to reach for the sky while they rummage through pockets for your wallet. Either way, you're not much closer to Toronto.

Needless to say, Trevor and I guessed incorrectly at countless intersections. On one occasion we found ourselves travelling the wrong direction along an expensive toll road—a road we could not afford to take. The only way to regain the free road without paying a toll would have been to cross a steep concrete ditch and four lanes of busy highway, and then drive against the flow of traffic on a busy off-ramp.

Now that I see it in writing, I can't believe we considered it. Indeed, Trevor dismissed the idea because of the "impossible" traverse across the ditch … a traverse I personally considered feasible. An intense argument erupted over whether or not we could even make the crossing, an argument that continued long after we'd agreed on the stupidity of the manoeuvre. It was a moot point. When the fight ended, we continued along the toll road.

But I had a moot point to prove. When I saw a break in traffic, I rode toward the ditch. Standing on my pegs to lower the bike's centre of gravity, I charged off the road and down the steep gradient like a stuntman in a James Bond movie. My front suspension compressed violently when I bottomed out. After taking a second to recover, I accelerated hard out of the ditch toward the oncoming traffic. I rode back through the ditch a bit faster on the return trip, bottoming out the suspension again and flashing Trevor a look that clearly said, "I told you so."

In spite of the heat, an icy silence hung between us when we stopped for lunch. I wanted to ask the waitress for a different glass, but I didn't know the right word and Trevor had the Spanish dictionary ... which is why I ended up asking her for a different penis.

Ah, such fun with the language barrier. Of course, not every misunderstanding proved so entertaining, or harmless. Often times, Trevor and I would stop to inquire about the safety of a certain route only to walk away with diametrically opposed interpretations of the conversation. If Trevor heard, "Use this road. It is not dangerous," I might hear, "Don't use this road. It is dangerous."

Then again, in a region where the term "civil engineer" refers more to an engineer's temperament than their qualifications, every road was dangerous. For example, open excavations swallowed the road in spots, marked only by a couple of orange cones that forced you unexpectedly into oncoming traffic. Potholes capable of concealing small dogs peppered the pavement beside hummocks of asphalt scattered across the roads like speed bumps on steroids.

Furry black tarantulas and large snakes sunned themselves in our path.

And then, of course, there was the ever-present threat of bandits. Maybe that's why we breathed a little easier when we finally crossed the border into Costa Rica—the safest of all Latin American countries according to our Lonely Planet guide. To celebrate, we parked on a dirt pullout in the shade of a Ceiba tree to enjoy a Bimbo (a Twinkie-like pastry without the filling). Two police officers in a sputtering white truck approached as Trevor and I nibbled at our Bimbos.

"Is everything all right?" the driver asked.

We nodded.

"You shouldn't stay here," he added, almost conversationally. "It's very dangerous."

"What? Why?" I asked.

"Bandits!" exclaimed the driver. "Very dangerous!" He playfully riddled me with bullets from an imaginary gun. "They come out of the jungle from Nicaragua." He pointed at the dense, bandit-concealing greenery that pressed against our bikes.

As soon as they left I strapped on my helmet and started the engine. Trevor, usually eager to eat and hesitant to ride, was several steps ahead of me, but even he could not match the haste of our friendly police officers, who had already fled the scene in a cloud of dust.

Of course, not all Central American police exist to serve and protect, as we discovered a couple of days later.

But first I should offer a little background. In Central America, all signs displaying posted speed limits are purely decorative. If you drive a hundred kilometres per hour in a sixty zone on an open highway, vehicles may slam into you from behind. Conversely, if you try driving the speed limit of seventy kilometres per hour on a precipitous mountain road, the mountain may spit you from its flanks like a fat kid ejecting watermelon seeds. We had grown accustomed to ignoring speed limits in favour of using common sense.

Inevitably, some cops clocked Trevor going a little fast one afternoon and pulled him over; I swear I could see dollar signs in their eyes when I drove in behind him. They made various threats in choppy English, accompanied by throat-slicing motions to accentuate their point.

"You see?" said the young cop (who bore a striking resemblance to Eric Estrada from *CHiPs*). He dragged his forefinger slowly across his throat. "Six months, no license, no drive."

The old cop said nothing, but frowned and shook his head as if to say, "This is a part of the job I hate."

The cops both started writing tickets very, very slowly. They looked up to see if we understood the gravity of the situation, and then continued writing.

"Or," the young cop said at last, pointing with his pen as if he'd just had an idea, "we could give you a warning."

"Yeah and how much does that cost?" I asked.

Trevor didn't wait for the reply. "That sounds good," he said. "We'll take the warning, then."

I carried two wallets for this very reason. One had all my money, identification, and credit cards. The other had a few dollars and fake ID. I opened the wallet containing a few dollars. "This is all we have," I lied. "We haven't been to the bank in Costa Rica yet."

Though disappointed, the police accepted our meagre offering and let us go. We obeyed all posted speed limits for the remainder of the day.

Unfortunately, obeying the law affords no exemption from the worst of all Central American travel hazards. Far worse than chaotic traffic, inadequate signage, massive potholes, language barriers, bandits, and corrupt police, nothing can compare to the real bane of motorcyclists—killer bees.

I'm not kidding.

By the time Trevor and I reached the Panamanian frontier, I had been stung too many times to count. If all the tiny bee stingers that pierced my skin while riding had been collected and neatly laid end to end, they would surely have encircled the globe seven times.

Seriously, how many times was I stung? Well, it's hard for me to nail down an exact number. I want to use the word *infinity*, but that's not really a number and it implies that the stinging had neither beginning nor end. Suffice it to say, entire armies of bees died while defending some perceived attack on their queen by two Canadian motorcyclists.

One particular incident stands out in my mind. The bee actually got into my helmet and became momentarily trapped between my sunglasses and my EYEBALL! As it buzzed furiously, fixated on my pupil like an archer on a bull's eye, I remained calm and said a quiet prayer (translation: I screamed like a little girl and nearly lost control of the bike in my attempt to rip the glasses from my face). It stands out in my mind mostly because the bee did *not* sting me. When you think about it, it's really a wonder we managed to stave off the effects of anaphylactic shock.

It's another wonder that Trevor and I safely added 8,000 kilometres to our odometers in two months, arriving in Panama City without having been kidnapped, sodomized, or killed. I thought about the doom-and-gloom travel advisories while relaxing in a hammock and drinking horrible Panamanian beer one afternoon. The advisories reminded me of an ancient Middle Eastern proverb: "The sluggard says, 'There is a lion outside!' or, 'I will be murdered in the streets!'" In other words, if one becomes obsessed with safety, he'll never leave the house.

Following several days of recuperation, we loaded our bikes for the return journey and waved goodbye to the local family we had been staying with. Trevor popped a little wheelie and roared through the gates of the compound to everyone's delight. Not to be outdone, I revved my engine to 5,000 rpms and dumped the clutch from a standing start, sending my front wheel rocketing skyward and my feet flailing wildly to the side. When my front end slammed back to earth, I waved to everyone like I meant to do that and rode away very carefully. For the first time in months we pointed our bikes in the direction of home and rode confidently on familiar roads, well aware of the hazards that lay before us.

Jeremy Kroeker lives in Calgary, Alberta. His mouth and brain operate independently of one another, which has caused him to do at least one outrageously stupid thing in more than twenty countries. He is currently working on a book about his motorcycle journey through Central America. Look for it this fall at www.trafford.com.

Arresting Scenery

A different kind of souvenir from paradise.

By Michelle Bland

I had been dreaming about postcard-perfect Hawaii for weeks: the sun, the sand, the warm tropical breeze slipping in off the Pacific. As a recruitment officer working for a private college in Illinois, it was my job to travel to such places to meet with potential students. And if I was forced to catch some sunshine and play a bit of beach Frisbee while there—to develop a comfortable rapport with the prospective students, of course—then so be it. Sometimes my job demanded such sacrifices.

I was ecstatic to learn that a friend of a friend, who happened to be traveling off-island at the time, had even given me permission to stay at her Maui condominium for a week. Not only would I have my airfare to Hawaii covered by the school, but I would have a private pad.

As anyone who has been to Maui knows, it is an enchanting place at any time of year, but even more so in November, when cold pre-winter winds are blowing in Illinois. This climate differential was not lost on me when I exited the airport and gulped my first breath of warm tropical air. I handed my taxi driver the address of the condo I was staying at, then sat back and gazed out my window as we drove past swaying palm trees and pedestrians in shorts and T-shirts.

The condominium did not disappoint. It was open and breezy and well furnished. On the kitchen table was a handwritten note from Bernice.

Hello Michelle, it said. *Please make yourself right at home. The keys to my Mercury are hanging in the front hall closet. Feel free to use it while you're here. Enjoy your stay! Kind regards, Bernice.*

That evening, after making an appointment with one of my potential students for the next day, I climbed behind the wheel of Bernice's Mercury and went for a little joyride. I detoured through downtown, getting a feel for the city's relaxed rhythm, then found a beach and went for a short walk. On the way home, I stopped at a service station and filled the car with gas.

The next day was as gloriously sunny as the day I had arrived, so I was eager to get going. I jumped into the Mercury and navigated through Maui's traffic to the home of the potential student I had spoken with the previous evening, a girl named Christina. She greeted me at the door wearing tan khaki shorts, a T-shirt, and a broad smile.

Over lunch at a Chinese buffet, we laughed and got to know one another. Christina was positive and enthusiastic, and it was easy to see that she was interested in our college. After lunch, we drove back to the condo to change into bathing suits and grab the Frisbee, suntan lotion, and beach towels. It was time for the formal interview ... accompanied by some sun, sand, and surf!

A couple of blocks from Bernice's condo, a police cruiser pulled up behind us. Absent-mindedly, I checked the speedometer and looked over to make sure Christina's seat belt was fastened. Everything looked fine, so you can imagine my surprise when a pair of red and blue flashers suddenly went off in the rear-view mirror.

I cautiously pulled over to the side of the road and leaned over to open the glove compartment, anticipating a random insurance and registration check. Suddenly, I heard a loud male voice booming over a megaphone: "GET YOUR HANDS AWAY FROM THE GLOVE COMPARTMENT! GET OUT OF THE CAR WITH YOUR HANDS IN THE AIR!"

I snatched my hand away from the glove compartment.

"GET OUT OF THE CAR WITH YOUR HANDS IN THE AIR!" the voice repeated.

Suddenly, several more squad cars appeared out of nowhere, squealing in from all directions to block off potential escape routes. I couldn't believe my eyes. When I looked over at Christina, hoping that she might have an answer, I was disappointed to find that she didn't. Her mouth was gaping as wide as my own.

"GET OUT OF THE CAR WITH YOUR HANDS IN THE AIR! THIS IS YOUR LAST WARNING!" the voice commanded again, this time a little more urgently. Obviously, this guy meant business. And it sounded like he was losing his patience with us.

So I undid my seatbelt, grabbed my purse, and cautiously opened the door. I climbed out of the Mercury and lifted my purse in the air, still assuming that they wanted to see a valid driver's license.

"DROP YOUR PURSE ON THE GROUND!" the cop shouted into his megaphone.

That's when I saw the guns for the first time. There were several of them, and they were all drawn and pointed directly at me, including one that was in the hands of a nervous young officer who looked to be in his twenties. He looked like he had just graduated from the cop shop, and he was kneeling behind the car, shaking like a hurricane-battered palm tree.

Recoiling, I dropped my purse on the pavement and stood rigidly, waiting with what might be described as a wee bit of trepidation for the cop's next instructions.

"WALK AROUND TO THE BACK AND PLACE YOUR HANDS ON TOP OF THE CAR!" shouted the cop. This guy was really starting to confuse and frighten me, but I obeyed, realizing that I didn't have many options.

"NOW, YOU IN THE PASSENGER SEAT! GET OUT OF THE CAR WITH YOUR HANDS IN THE AIR!"

I looked at Christina, who warily exited the car. She was in tears. The sight of her crying made me even more angry and frustrated. I started crying, too.

"Why are you doing this?" I wailed as the police officers approached from behind, grabbed my arms, and clicked handcuffs around my wrists.

"Do you understand that you're being arrested for grand theft auto?" asked a brusque policeman. But it wasn't so much a question as a statement.

"What do you mean?" I cried. "No, I don't understand! Please enlighten me!"

He ignored my pleas, and as a second officer put handcuffs on Christina, he began reading us our rights. "You have the right to remain silent. Anything you say can and will be used against you in a court of law. You have the right to an attorney...."

Then, all too quickly, we were head-ducked into the backs of separate squad cars and taken away.

At the Maui police station, they handcuffed me to a wall and led Christina into a separate room for interrogation. I sat there for an hour and a half, waiting and wondering what the hell I had gotten myself into.

Finally, they came to fetch me and gave me the opportunity to explain. I told the officer that I had arrived in Hawaii two days earlier, stayed at Bernice's condo, and taken Christina out for an afternoon of Chinese food and sunshine, explaining that my hostess had given us permission to use her Mercury.

"How could Bernice tell you that I stole her car?" I sobbed, completely drained. "She's not even in Hawaii right now!"

"The car you were driving belongs to a man," said the interrogating officer, looking a little perplexed as he jotted copious notes. "The owner of the car is a priest, actually."

"A priest?" I repeated, startled. "How can that be possible?"

"The car you were driving belongs to a priest," was all the officer said as he continued to scribble notes.

My story matched Christina's, of course, so after handcuffing me back to the wall, the police sent a squad car back to the condo to investigate. They found a clue. A big clue. It was another Mercury parked near the condo. It was not the same make or model, but when they tried Bernice's key in the lock, the door mysteriously opened. When they tried the key in the ignition, the car mysteriously started.

"Well, I'll be damned!" one can imagine the investigating officer saying. "This key works in two different cars ... in the same parking lot. I wonder what the odds of that are?"

One can also imagine a somewhat confused priest, having noticed his car missing the previous evening, reacting with surprise when it is returned an hour later with a full tank of gas.

So the Maui police let us go, a little embarrassed by the whole episode, but not particularly apologetic. To make up for the terrible misunderstanding, they were gracious enough to fingerprint us and take our mug shots. I can't say that I'm entirely displeased. I mean, how often do you get to be a criminal for a day? And not many tourists in Hawaii get souvenirs like the one I received: several black-and-white photos of a red-eyed, tear-stained girl holding a number in front of her chest.

Michelle Bland is currently pursuing a life-long dream to work as a schoolteacher and part-time trapper in rural Alaska. She says the beaches aren't as nice, but the bone-chilling temperatures and clouds of ravenous mosquitoes more than make up for it. And she hasn't been arrested once.

Trans-Canada Christmas

A family tries to create Yuletide cheer on the open road.

By Kathy Chiasson

It was the middle of December in 1977 when my husband Euclyde, our three daughters and I left Cape Breton Island for a return to life on the opposite side of Canada. Our destination was the small city of Victoria on the balmy West Coast, a mere six thousand kilometres distant.

We had ended up on Cape Breton purely by accident. Although Euclyde is a francophone who grew up in eastern Canada, my family were westerners who had lived in British Columbia for many years. Euclyde and I met in western Canada, and we liked it there. We never intended to leave.

But the best-laid plans sometimes take unexpected detours. Euclyde was offered training and what sounded like a dream job with Canada's Atomic Energy Agency in Quebec, but shortly after the training ended, the company misplaced the job. They told us that we would have to move to Cape Breton Island. No sooner had we moved to the East Coast than the promised dream job failed to materialize yet again. My dear husband took a contract position with a company in Algeria and held it for two months before he decided that working abroad was not for a family man.

We had already decided that we would move our family back to British Columbia if the job did not work out, and Victoria was the best choice because our family and friends were there to offer a support network that would help us get back on our feet. So that's where we decided to go.

But first we had to get there.

Euclyde spotted an advertisement for an old sixty-six-passenger Bluebird school bus in our local paper, and after looking at the bus, we purchased it for $1,500. We packed all our worldly belongings inside and departed ten days before Christmas. Our goal was to get to Victoria just before the holidays so that our daughters could enjoy a relatively normal Christmas among family and friends.

I should say that navigating six thousand kilometres of frozen asphalt in the middle of winter would be an adventure for even the most hardened road warrior. Now imagine doing it in a decrepit old school bus that after three days of packing was crammed to the rafters with furniture, toys, bicycles, appliances—not to mention a steamer trunk filled with my fine china.

The Bluebird was so stuffed with our worldly possessions that our oldest daughter, ten-year-old Renée, had to sit on a kitchen chair wedged behind the driver's seat. I sat on another chair in the middle of the aisle, while four-year-old Celeste and five-year-old Nicole shared the front seat on the passenger's side.

On the morning of our departure, the weather was stable and the roads were in surprisingly good condition. We took it as a good omen. Maybe six thousand kilometres of winter driving wouldn't be so bad after all. The old school bus creaked across the floating bridge to the mainland, and we were on our way, buoyed by the promise of a new life. We passed through the villages of New Scotland—Antigonish, New Glasgow, Pictou—and watched the Eastern Highlands shrink gradually into flat farmland.

The first trouble didn't appear until the next morning, when in Moncton, New Brunswick, I slipped on some ice in a motel parking lot and fell on my wrist. My left hand soon looked like a snowmobile mitten, swelling so badly that my wedding ring started cutting off circulation to my finger.

Then the muffler fell off the bus and the alternator died.

"My God, how are we ever going to get to Victoria?" I muttered. "We're less than five hundred kilometres west of Cape Breton."

Euclyde didn't say much. We both knew that without an alternator, the bus wasn't going to make it across the province, let alone the country.

The good news is that we weren't far from Fredericton, a small regal city in New Brunswick where Euclyde's sister Rita lives. We limped into the city just before the bus died. When Rita saw my swollen hand, she whisked me to the hospital's emergency ward to have my wedding ring cut off.

Fortunately for me (and for my ring), liberal applications of olive oil and a good deal of persistence managed the task. By pure chance, Rita's husband Don happened to work for the local school board—and of course, had the necessary connections to repair the bus. But we were still stuck in town for the next two days while we waited for him to finish the repairs.

The Trans-Canada Highway then led us relentlessly west through New Brunswick, Quebec, and Canada's capital city of Ottawa until we reached the Great Lakes. In those days, this section of the Trans-Canada was narrow and winding and very exposed to severe winter storms; it snaked ominously through the mountainous country of the Canadian Shield. Euclyde checked the weather forecast in Sudbury and found warnings that winter storms were brewing in both eastern and western Canada. But at that moment, the forecast for the Lakehead (the stretch of highway between Sault Ste. Marie and Thunder Bay) looked clear. We decided to go for it.

It was somewhere along Superior's remote north shore—exactly where I can't remember—that the bus started running low on fuel. We passed service station after service station with *CLOSED FOR THE SEASON* signs posted out front, and our situation started to look pretty grim.

Finally, we found a service station that had a car idling in the parking lot. We pulled up to a gas pump just as a man was closing the front door. It turned out that he was leaving for the season, and wouldn't have returned until the following spring. His family was in the car, the car was running, and he was turning the key in the lock.

"You're lucky we hadn't left," he said, shaking his head. "You'd never have made it across the Lakehead without filling up here."

Graciously, he opened the front door, turned on a gas pump, and filled our thirsty Bluebird until she couldn't drink another drop.

When Euclyde pulled back onto the highway, I leaned over and—not without a trace of irony—asked, "You know that old saying about God looking after fools and children?"

My husband nodded.

"Well, you and I aren't children."

Our morning routine usually started with eating cold cereal on the bus, which would satisfy our hunger pangs until we found a restaurant. This worked perfectly well until we reached the cold, clear skies of Manitoba, arguably the most wintry province in all of Canada.

Manitoba had just been hit by an ice storm, and as we drove through a beautiful and surreal landscape cloaked in ice, we stared in disbelief at trees that looked like giant Freezies. As we approached Winnipeg, we discovered that extreme cold had caused the surface of the highway to contract, creating large trenches that ran across its width. Apparently, the front and rear wheels of the bus were exactly the wrong distance apart, because the bus was soon lurching up and down in the air like a rodeo horse. I cringed as I imagined my fine china being smashed to pieces.

Celeste spilled the milk from her cereal on the floor, and as we watched, it quickly drained down the side and pooled on the steps leading up from the front doors of the bus. It froze in place there as the incessant lurching of the bus continued. Then Euclyde narrowly escaped injury as he exited the bus and nearly wiped out on the frozen milk. It was Christmas Eve.

We made it as far as Virden, Manitoba before evening fell. Euclyde pulled into the parking lot of a MacLeod's department store, but couldn't find a place to park where he wouldn't be blocking traffic. So I jumped out, taking great care to leap over the skating rink of frozen milk, and ran into the store. In half an hour I managed all my Christmas shopping. I even bought some tinsel and a few decorations for a potted fern that would serve as our Christmas tree. That night we sat around the festive fern and sang Christmas carols as Euclyde drove. After the girls had finally drifted off to sleep, I quietly wrapped presents while sitting on my kitchen chair in the aisle of the great Bluebird bus.

At around ten o'clock that evening, we drifted into Balgonie, Saskatchewan, a small hamlet a few kilometres east of Regina. "This looks pretty good," said Euclyde as he inched the bus down the narrow street looking for a motel.

We spotted a couple walking along the sidewalk toward one of the units. "I hope there's not a party brewing," I said to Euclyde.

"I don't think we'll have any trouble with them," he said. "They're senior citizens."

I took a closer look and saw a man who looked well into his seventies. He even had a walker to help him shuffle along. His wife was not much younger.

At shortly after two in the morning, Euclyde and I were roused from our motel bed to the sound of smashing glass. The voice of an angry man was easily discernible from the unit next door. Perhaps the old man was in a festive mood, and was proffering Christmas cheer to his wife.

We endured the pitched argument for several long minutes, and just as Euclyde was about to check on the bus, the fighting ended as suddenly as it had begun. Then there was silence. Eventually we drifted back to sleep, grateful that our daughters hadn't been roused from slumber.

When we reached Calgary the next afternoon, the two younger girls and I decided that enough was enough. Euclyde dropped us at the airport hotel, where we bought plane tickets to Vancouver for the next day. Euclyde and Renée would continue in the bus, and the two youngest girls and I would fly to the coast. I called our friends Wally and Violet to let them know we'd be arriving in Vancouver at noon, and to ask if one of them could pick us up. "I'm cooking Christmas dinner for you," Violet told me, "so don't be late."

That night, Euclyde and Renée were so excited about finally arriving in British Columbia that they couldn't have slept even if they'd wanted to—so they just kept driving. As Euclyde described it to me after we were reunited, the full moon cast a silvery glow across the snow-clad peaks, causing them to radiate a faint pastel blue. It was one of the most beautiful things they had ever seen.

For breakfast, they had chocolate cake on the bus, figuring they'd surprise us at the airport.

They arrived at the airport more than an hour before our flight landed, as did Wally. All three of them were there to greet us when we got off the plane. Before long, Euclyde and Renée departed on the bus; the rest of us piled our luggage in the back of Wally's car and headed for the ferry terminal. The Strait of Georgia was the last obstacle we would face before reaching the Promised Land.

Then Wally made a wrong turn. By the time he had circled back to the ticket window to purchase a ticket, the afternoon ferry had finished boarding. And Euclyde and Renée were on board.

"You'll have to wait two hours for the next ferry," the lady at the ticket window told us. The ferry was still sitting in its berth, so I pleaded with her to make an exception this one time, but she didn't particularly care about our cross-country ordeal. Or the fact that we would now be two hours late for our turkey dinner.

We finally made it to Vancouver Island, a little behind schedule, but in one piece. Our friend Margaret had offered to let us leave the bus at her house, so Euclyde drove off to park it while the children and I continued on to Wally and Violet's home, hungry and exhausted.

A long time passed without Euclyde showing up, and I began to worry, wondering if he had somehow gotten lost. Finally he arrived, looking more than a little worse for wear.

What had actually happened was somewhat worse than getting lost. Euclyde had found Margaret's home without incident, but as he pulled onto the shoulder to park the bus, he felt a sinking feeling in his gut. Or was it the entire bus that was sinking?

He quickly shifted the bus into reverse and tried to back out, but a pair of mud-slicks shot out from under the front tires. Driving forward proved equally ineffective. The bus was so heavily loaded with furniture and appliances that as soon as he had driven onto the wet soil at the side of the road, the bus had started to sink. And it didn't stop sinking until the mud reached the wheel wells.

"... But all our belongings!" I stammered after he finished relating his defeat at the hands of the West Coast mud.

"Don't worry," he reassured me. "Everything will be fine. But I think the bus is going to be sitting in Margaret's boulevard for a while."

And that's when my dear husband did what any man who had just driven an old school bus six thousand kilometres on winter roads with his wife and three children, only to have it get stuck in two feet of mud, would do. He took off his jacket and his mud-stained hat, sat down at the table and ate some turkey.

Kathy Chiasson and her family have lived in Victoria for almost thirty years. They remember this trip as one of their greatest family adventures.

Drive-away Honeymoon

The honeymoon was great. Getting home was the hard part.

By Curtis Foreman

When you're driving north in a repossessed vehicle along a frozen highway and your wife is trying to extinguish a fire in the back seat, it can be easy to forget that you're on your honeymoon.

But I suppose I'm getting ahead of myself.

Janna and I met in the summer of 1996 and it wasn't long before we fell in love. We were living west of Prince George, British Columbia and working at summer jobs—me in the woods with a forty-pound brush saw, Janna at the Grand Trunk Inn slinging beers for loggers and tree planters. She brought me a Guinness, we smiled at each other, and six months later we were married.

We found an apartment in Kerrisdale, Vancouver's "blue hair district," and spent the next couple of years scrambling to make ends meet. A honeymoon was out of the question, but we still wanted one. So, when I graduated from university in the spring of 1998, we decided to move back up north for the summer, sock away some money, and then treat ourselves to a wild road trip of a honeymoon. I got back on with my old tree-spacing crew and was soon slogging through clearcuts, while Janna found a job with a highway crew. We banked our earnings and worked extra shifts. At the end of the summer, we plotted a course for Mexico.

The honeymoon was a dream come true. As we had heard—and soon learned for ourselves—a Canadian dollar goes a long way in Mexico. We rented a beautiful hotel room for a month in a little town south of Acapulco, with a balcony overlooking the rolling Pacific. Every day was a romantic adventure. We took day trips, surfed, wrote, danced, met other travellers, and made friends with the locals. We swam in the breakers every morning before breakfast and dined out three times a day.

The money started running low after about a month and a half, so with considerable reluctance, we began making plans to return home.

In early November, we hitched a ride north with an artist we had met, then took a bus over the border at Nogales into Arizona. Our money situation was getting a bit tight, so after some discussion, we decided to drop in at the nearest auto drive-away office, which was headquartered in Phoenix.

An auto drive-away is an experience everyone should try at least once in their life. Here's how it works: pretty much every major city in the United States has an office that delivers cars to other cities. At any given time you can walk into one of these offices and find cars to be delivered to Florida, New York, Los Angeles, and so on. You pick your destination city, sign a waiver, pay a deposit, swear on your grandmother's grave to deliver the car in one piece and on time—and for the price of gas money, you're a driver!

I'd had great fortune with drive-aways, delivering new cars from California to Washington, Washington to Texas, and more. However, it seemed that fortune was nowhere to be found in Phoenix.

"We've got a car going to Oregon," said the woman at the counter, "but it's not exactly in great shape. The owner died a few months back and her boyfriend took off with the car and stopped making lease payments. We just got it back from the cops this week. You want to take a look at it?"

I shot Janna a questioning look.

"Sure," she said. "Why not?"

The car was a white convertible Geo Tracker, and it was in utter disrepair. The body was so dented and scratched that I wondered if the vehicle had been rolled. The soft top was completely shredded, as were the seats, which had stuffing hanging out of the sides. A few bare wires dangled from the space originally inhabited by the stereo.

"The police found it abandoned up a gravel road," the drive-away woman explained, with a look that was at once apologetic and hopeful. "No sign of the boyfriend. We need to get it back to the bank in Klamath Falls, up in Oregon."

"Does it run?" I asked, staring with bewilderment at the wreckage before us.

"Oh yes," she exclaimed, her face brightening. "We drove it here from the police station. And we had all the upholstery steam cleaned too, in case you're wondering."

"I *was* wondering," I said. "Give us a minute."

She went back into the office and left Janna and me scratching our heads and staring at the pathetic little vehicle. The sun was setting and we were standing in a parking lot in Phoenix, half a continent away from home, with a couple of huge backpacks and just a few hundred dollars to our name.

"You up for it?" I asked.

"Let's do it," said Janna.

We signed the papers and took the keys from the beaming drive-away woman, then threw our packs in the back and did our best to zip up the torn soft top. "That thing will need some duct tape before we hit the freeway," said Janna as we climbed into the dilapidated seats.

I nodded and jammed the key into the ignition. The starter turned over grudgingly a few times before the little engine fired to life. The exhaust was shockingly loud, and I guessed that the pipe and muffler were either damaged or missing altogether. I carefully buckled my seat belt and backed up. A few seconds later we roared onto the highway north of town, followed by a wispy trail of bluish smoke.

As we approached the freeway, I noticed that the on-ramp sloped steeply uphill. I downshifted and floored the gas pedal with no discernable result, other than a startling increase in the volume of smoke belching from the rear of the vehicle. Someone behind me honked their horn.

We cruised onto the ramp at about sixty-five kilometres an hour, gradually slowing as we climbed the grade. I wondered if we would make it, but the Tracker seemed to find its preferred pace at about thirty kilometres an hour, and we finished the climb at that speed. Traffic rushed past us on the left, and I crept along toward the end of the merge lane, frantically looking for a break in the traffic.

With increasing desperation, I pumped the gas pedal, searching for some kind of a "sweet spot" that would yield a bit of acceleration. There didn't seem to be one. As we approached the end of the merge lane, I checked my mirror and noticed with alarm that the smoke pouring from the back of the vehicle was actually obscuring my view of the lane I was trying to merge into.

The rush of vehicles beside us stopped, and I realized they were probably hanging back, hesitant to enter our smokescreen. Crossing my fingers, I signalled and changed lanes, noticing with some relief that the climb had ended and the road was beginning to descend. The smoke behind us thinned and the Tracker accelerated to an acceptable highway speed. We settled in and did our best to enjoy the ride, despite glares coming from the folks who passed us in the fast lane.

If you're wondering, yes, this was how we merged into highway traffic every time—unless we were lucky enough to find a downward-sloping on-ramp.

An hour or so after leaving Phoenix, Janna shouted something I didn't quite hear over the din of the engine, highway noise, and merciless flapping of the soft top.

"What?" I yelled.

"I said, let's find some tape and seal up the top," she shouted back.

We pulled over and bought tape, food, and cigarettes at a gas station. After making suitable attempts to patch up the worst of the damage, we cruised up another on-ramp, waited for a break in traffic, and then resumed our journey north amid the ever-present cloud of smoke.

Janna opened a pack of Marlboros and pushed in the cigarette lighter, which stayed put long enough to heat up, and then ejected forcefully from the dash, bouncing off the centre console and into the back seat. Wide-eyed, Janna clicked out of her seat belt and turned around to retrieve the hot lighter, which was rolling around in the back among our groceries.

An acrid smell of burning vinyl began to waft through the drafty cabin of the vehicle. "I can't reach it!" she shouted. "It's burning the seat!" I wondered if I should pull over before the fire began to spread.

"Ow!" she cried, now wedged between the driver and passenger seats, her foot on the dash as she fished around for the lighter. "It's burning me!" I put my signal on and peered into the rear-view mirror for cars following in our smokescreen as I prepared for an emergency stop.

Flailing after the lighter, Janna accidentally kicked my hand, and for a sickening second we lurched sideways into the left-hand lane. I had a horrible vision of hitting a transport truck and watching my wife fly ass-first through the windshield with her hair on fire.

"Got it," she shouted as I regained control and returned to the centre of our lane. She flopped back into her seat, sucking her singed fingers. "The hell with this goddamn thing," she cursed, dropping it into the glove box.

Our eyes met. I took in her furious glare, she my wide-eyed panic. We drove on in silence until I noticed she was giggling. Within a few minutes, we were laughing uncontrollably.

Over the next few days, as we travelled north through California, I grew accustomed to the Tracker's pathetic engine. I raced downhill wherever possible to gather momentum, then geared down and crawled up hills with the hazard lights flashing while big rigs honked at our smokescreen and passed us in second gear.

To amuse ourselves, Janna and I shouted stories to each other over the incessant noise. When we grew hoarse, we would sit in silence and watch the hills and valleys and forests of California creep slowly past. One morning, we stopped for breakfast at a café and noticed an advertisement for two ranch hands to work on a large estate; the place looked gorgeous in the photos.

"Why are we going home?" Janna asked.

"I'm not entirely sure," I said truthfully. "Are we up for another gamble?"

Simultaneously, we turned our eyes to the Tracker, then back to one another.

"Good point," said Janna. "You driving?"

It was late fall, and the weather in Oregon was bitterly cold. On our last day in the Tracker we drove into a light blizzard, which intensified as we ploughed ahead toward our destination; snowflakes swirled inside the drafty little cabin of the vehicle. We put on all the clothing we had, noticing with a mixture of amusement and alarm that despite the tepid breeze emitting from the cranked heater, snow was actually accumulating in drifts against our backpacks in the back seat.

Eventually we pulled into Klamath Falls in southern Oregon and delivered the car to the bank, our ears ringing from the noise of the exhaust and torn top. The bank manager insisted on inspecting the vehicle before returning our security deposit; in the parking lot, she shook her head incredulously and asked, "You two made it here from Arizona in this thing?"

We nodded.

"You're lucky to be alive," she said.

We nodded again, in full agreement.

We spent the last of our money on a couple of bus tickets to Vancouver, and the final thirty-six hours of our trip passed in a sleepless blur of snow-covered highways. As they say, the honeymoon was over.

Janna and I split up a few years ago; she now works as a hiking guide in northern BC and the Yukon, and I'm still living in the city.

But when we see each other, we share a few laughs over what was undoubtedly one of the most bizarre honeymoon adventures a couple has ever had.

Curtis Foreman once rode a motorcycle with no headlight halfway through the Rocky Mountains at night, and he has never been the same since. When not editing travel literature or writing ad copy, he can be found on a snowboard, mountain bike or laying on a warm stretch of beach sand. He lives in Vancouver, British Columbia.

The Great Mother's Day Race

Pulling out all the stops for Mom.

By John Judd

It was six o'clock on a Saturday morning when I rolled into Fort MacLeod, Alberta. I had left British Columbia's south-central interior the previous afternoon, and sixteen hours of driving had me nodding my head at the wheel. My eyes were bloodshot. My ears were ringing. I was big time overdrawn at the sleep bank, but making a deposit anytime soon wasn't very likely.

I still had thirty-two hours of driving ahead of me.

That's when I spotted two hitchhikers standing on the road ahead. One was a tall, rangy blonde fellow; the other was short and stocky and sported a thick black beard. They looked a little rough around the edges, but I was getting desperate.

I slowed the car, pulled onto the shoulder, and rolled down my window. "Can you drive?" I asked the tall fellow.

"Yeah, I can drive."

"I'm going to southern Ontario. Where are you headed?"

"Anywhere but here," they said in unison.

And with that I handed over the car keys. I hopped out of the driver's seat, climbed into the back, and promptly fell asleep.

It wasn't until five hours later, when I woke up west of Regina, that I found out the hitchhikers had just been released from prison.

*   *   *

My journey across Canada started rather innocently. I had been sitting at my parents' home in Osoyoos, British Columbia, in early May when the phone rang. It was my Uncle Jack calling from Barrie, Ontario. He had a job offer. "We need a strapping young lad to work in our cement factory," he said. "Are you interested?" The job largely consisted of hauling and piling concrete blocks onto skids in a warehouse.

I was unemployed at the time, a 22-year-old with a serious case of wanderlust. I was particularly in love with my little 1966 Pontiac Persian convertible—a beaut of a car! It had served me well on many road trips, including one memorable journey down the California coast with my brother Tom and cousin Bob. We did that trip during spring break, spelling each other off at the wheel, cruising for twenty-four hours with the top down to reach San Diego. At one point Tom was sitting on the back of the car with a blanket wrapped around him while I was clocking about 120 kilometres an hour. In an instant the blanket sagged, the wind caught it, and Tom was almost pulled off the back of the car. After that incident, nobody sat on the back of the car while we were driving on the highway.

Despite my wanderlust, I had a good work ethic and making money to pay for future trips was high on my priority list. Even though it didn't sound like the most glamorous work, I accepted my uncle's job offer with gratitude, and hung up the phone.

When I told my parents, the first words out of my mother's mouth were, "That's wonderful news, honey. Do you think you'll be there in time for Mother's Day dinner?" I had nearly forgotten. My mother was flying to Ontario the next day to visit my grandmother for the weekend. And she had already made dinner reservations at Barrie's Continental Hotel for seven on Sunday evening.

I have to admit, the idea of an epic cross-country race against time really inspired the road warrior in me. I packed my suitcase, loaded up my little convertible, and assured my mother I would be in Barrie for dinner. I don't think she believed me. I pulled out of my parent's driveway at two on Friday afternoon, feeling energized. Forty-eight hours of driving lay ahead of me. The Great Mother's Day Race was on.

*   *   *

The hitchhikers and I stopped in Regina for dinner. It turns out Chad and Jason were drifters—not hardened criminals—who had been put in prison for vagrancy. After eating, I stopped at a department store to buy a shirt and tie for Sunday. Then we pressed on toward Manitoba.

The three of us took turns driving. I was asleep when we reached Winnipeg, so I didn't notice Jason miss the exit for the bypass route around the city. As a result, we ended up wasting precious time trying to navigate through the downtown area without a map. We finally found the Trans-Canada Highway heading east, and an hour later we left the Prairies behind, entering the dark foreboding landscape of the Canadian Shield.

It wasn't until two a.m. on Sunday morning that we finally pulled into Kenora, the first sizable town in western Ontario. I asked Chad and Jason to fill up with gas and check the oil while I ran to the washroom. We still had to drive across Canada's largest province in the dark, and with all the moose crossing the highway we had to be careful. But every minute counted, so we had to keep driving.

At around six a.m., less than an hour west of Thunder Bay, the convertible's engine made a horrible sound like fingers grating against a chalkboard. Then it seized and stopped. I was driving up a steep hill at the time, so I put the car in neutral and coasted backward down the road and into the parking lot of a gas station. Steam was billowing from the engine.

I wasn't sure what to do, so I waited disconsolately until the owner came out and told us he wouldn't be opening for another hour. A forlorn Chad admitted he had forgotten to check the oil in Kenora, which is why the engine had burned up. He felt terrible, but not as terrible as I did. I was devastated. It looked like the race was over.

After Gus, the service station owner, had looked at the car, he proclaimed it unfixable. There was nothing we could do but wait for the RCMP to arrive and give us a lift into Thunder Bay.

When I told the officer my sad story he offered to drop me at the airport, and it was only then that I realized the race wasn't over. Checking flights at the airport confirmed the first available plane arrived at Pearson International in Toronto at just after five p.m.. I promptly bought a ticket, arranged for a rental car at the other end, and waited.

My flight arrived in Toronto on time, but when I went to look for my luggage I couldn't find it. I waited patiently at the conveyor belt—and then not so patiently—all the while glancing at my wristwatch. The other passengers on my flight picked up their bags and dispersed one by one. Eventually the conveyor belt stopped spitting out luggage onto the carousel; my suitcase was still nowhere in sight.

This was definitely not my day!

I asked the airline staff about my bag, pleading with them to find it quickly as I was late for an important meeting. At first they didn't have any idea where it might be, but after an hour of searching they finally found it. For some reason it had been placed on a "fragile items" cart.

I dashed out of the airport to the car rental office, filled out the necessary paperwork and then floored it all the way to Barrie. Everybody else was driving at the same reckless speed, so I wasn't worried about getting a ticket.

I arrived at the Continental Hotel at eight, an hour late for Mother's Day dinner. But it didn't really matter. Everyone was still at the restaurant, and I had quite the story to share over dessert.

If my mother's glowing expression was anything to go by, there's no question who had won the race.

John Judd worked at the cement factory for several weeks, ruining three pairs of jeans in the process. He later got a job working at the Mansfield Tire plant doing maintenance during the summer shutdown. It was at a staff BBQ hosted by his boss that he met Patti, the boss's daughter, who later became his wife. John now works in the oil and gas industry, splitting his time between Calgary and Fort McMurray, Alberta.

Do you have a Great Story?

If you enjoyed this collection of stories and feel you have an outrageous, funny, heartwarming or inspirational tale that you would like to share, we would love to hear from you. Our only rules are that your story has some unusual, illuminating or humorous twist to it, that it's a true anecdote and that it has something to do with travel.

We are already working on a follow-up to *I Sold My Gold Tooth for Gas Money* and we can accept either story outlines or pieces that have already been written. You don't have to be a professional writer. We look forward to hearing from anybody that has a great yarn to spin.

To obtain more detailed submission guidelines, please visit Summit Studios on our web site at:

www.summitstudios.biz

Please submit stories or story outlines by e-mail, fax or snail mail to:

SUMMIT STUDIOS
#105, 2572 Birch St.
Vancouver, BC V6H 2T4
Fax: (778) 371-8561
E-mail: submissions@summitstudios.biz

We look forward to hearing from you.

Acknowledgements

A very special thanks to my fianceé, Stacey, who shares my passion for travel and the outdoors. Her unconditional support and her belief in my dream to found a publishing company have made this book possible.

Thanks to my family and friends who have offered ideas, support, and critical feedback as this book has taken shape.

Thanks to Curtis Foreman and Yvonne Jeffery for help with the editing, and to Kirk Seton for a great book design.

And finally, thanks to the many travellers who have contributed their stories to this book. Your willingness to share means that all of us are a little richer.

About Matt Jackson

A graduate of Wilfrid Laurier's Business Administration program, Matt Jackson was lured away from the corporate world by the thrill of adventure journalism while still a university student. He is now an author, photojournalist and professional speaker, and is the president of Summit Studios, a publishing company specializing in books about travel and the outdoors.

Matt's first book, *The Canada Chronicles: A Four-Year Hitchhiking Odyssey*, won the IPPY award for best North American travel memoir in 2004. His work has also been featured in more than two dozen popular magazines including *Equinox*, *Explore*, *Photo Life*, *Canadian Geographic* and *BBC Wildlife*. He currently lives in Vancouver.